.

Be Still and Know

Be Still and Know

Psalm 46 and the *Stinkin' Stuff* of Life

↜

Stuart H. Schwartz

RESOURCE *Publications* · Eugene, Oregon

Table of Contents

Acknowledgements vii

Chapter 1 Psalm 46: We Are Not Alone 1

Chapter 2 A Doctor Speaks, a Body Speaks, God Speaks 11

Chapter 3 Faith and Donuts 25

Chapter 4 Jew Ain't Kidding! 37

Chapter 5 Hell, I Tell You 47

Chapter 6 More Hell, More Abuse 58

Chapter 7 Déjà Vu All Over Again 74

Chapter 8 Rape . . . and Hope 85

Chapter 9 Abortion: Thank God for Forgiveness 95

Chapter 10 A Last Lesson 106

Chapter 11 Psalm 46: Be Still, Be Loved, Be Strong 115

Epilogue 119

Acknowledgements

WORDS FAIL WHEN EXPRESSING the depth of my love for the two women who were kind enough to accept my marriage proposals. Although there is no accounting for their taste in doing so, I am both honored and blessed by these partners in life. Sharon—who this book is about—and I had more than three decades together before ALS struck. A year after her passing Victoria was foolish enough to marry me. She has been with me every step of the way as I wrote this book, and caregiver in my long battle with cancer. Her feedback—on not just the book, but life—has been invaluable. She is the rare individual who can see and understand both the big picture and the smallest of details, a woman of encouragement and context. Our love is deep and enduring, as was and is my love with Sharon, whose bravery and cheer and faith in the face of certain death is the subject of this book. Both are women of faith. Both share a deep-rooted Judeo-Christian morality, and both are Christians in the best and original sense of the word. The Jewish sense of the word.

I use present tense here in reference to Sharon because she remains alive, both in my mind and in that mystery we call heaven.

Sharon's graceful (emotionally, if not physically—for ALS is a wasting disease) and God-filled exit from this world allowed those left behind to continue our lives, free of the debilitating grief and guilt that so many of the living experience after the death of a loved one, or in dealing with debilitating disease (both physical and psychological). Sharon, with our last conversations, added new and

vii

discerning depth to my relationship with our daughters Chelsea and Brittany. And ultimately, healing.

Funny thing: As our faith grows, so does our capacity for understanding, patience, and the blessings of perseverance and love. Sharon's world. She wanted me to keep on walking, and use her lessons—beginning with "Be still and know"—to grow as a husband ("God will again bring someone into your life—he knows you need someone to keep you going in the right direction") and father ("You'll be a father all your life, everyday growing into different and more comfortable father").

My thanks and love to our daughters, Brittany and Chelsea. By observation, they taught me much about grief, which comes in many colors and tastes. Heartache is not one-size-fits-all. They have grown into very different adults. I've learned—again, thanks to Sharon—to love them in very different ways. Be still, and be patient.

Speaking of love: Our ability to give in love defines us as humans. I thank my brother, Robert, who was willing to donate his stem cells to keep me going; and I especially thank my sister, Trudy, the better match, who donated her stem cells for my second and ultimately successful transplant. She and her husband, Bob, in action and word, embody giving and loving. They are impressive in their good works, giving generously of themselves in helping disadvantaged youths. Family. Great stuff.

I'm thankful for the medical expertise and caring of the doctors and staff at the University of Virginia Health centers, the premiere academic medical center in the state of Virginia. And the care offered by the cancer center in Lynchburg. These medical professionals have blessed many lives . . . including mine.

And I'm also grateful for the ALS Association, which provides an amazing amount of support for patients and families suffering through this disease. Professional associations, organized around chronic and terminal diagnoses, are invaluable resources for patients and caregivers.

ACKNOWLEDGEMENTS

Speaking of blessings: I'm blessed by daughters and grandchildren aplenty. So many unique personalities, so many different approaches to life, so many unique relationships.

Last word: This book answers the question I'd been asked so many times over the years, "Why does Sharon smile so much?"

Now you know.

Psalm 46: We Are Not Alone

ALS, Faith, and Psalm 46

"THIS IS AS BAD as it gets."

Those were the words of one doctor when my late wife, Sharon, was diagnosed with ALS, a fatal neurodegenerative illness popularly known as Lou Gehrig's Disease.

"Yes, it *is* as bad as it gets," agreed Sharon later, dying from ALS. "It's torture by disease. But I have a counter to the bad: Faith. Faith that pulls, through Ps 46 and the Spirit, the good and strength and love of God."[1]

She looked at me, eyes moist. "And I will really, really need that strength."

This book was originally written some years ago, in draft form, shortly after she succumbed to ALS, amyotrophic lateral sclerosis. The disease affects nerve cells in the brain and spinal cord. One by one, the muscles that control walking, talking, and breathing wither away, leaving a mind trapped within a dying body and, ultimately, suffocation. The disease is terminal. Period. The end.

---

1. "Ps" here is a standard abbreviation for "Psalm." This is used throughout the book, except at the beginnings of sentences or in chapter and section titles.

It was a heartrending journey, one faced in varying degrees and with a multitude of symptoms by more than 135 million Americans with chronic, incurable diseases. Some go quickly; others live for years, with all experiencing, at one time or another, pain, suffering, and dread. For most of those afflicted—and ALS is only a tiny percentage of this group—that underlying sense of dread periodically surfaces as despair. There is nothing that so quickly robs patients and loved ones of joy as struggling with chronic and terminal illnesses. Pain hurts—that's why it's called "pain."

Some bear up under the strain of coping with illness better than others. They don't just survive, but thrive within the constraints of disease, treatment, and—for some—inexorable death. What is the difference? Faith. Scientific studies have repeatedly confirmed that faith, and especially Christian faith, makes a difference. Belief in God, belief in a God who loves and cares, in Jesus Christ—the loving, encouraging presence of that God—offers hope despite the facts on the ground, so to speak.

The Mayo Clinic summarized it this way: "Most studies have shown that religious involvement and spirituality are associated with better health outcomes, including greater longevity, coping skills, and health-related quality of life (even during terminal illness) and less anxiety, depression, and suicide." Across the board, in medical schools and hospitals, researchers have found that faith in general, and Christian faith in particular, eases the journey of a patient with a fatal or chronic disease.

This, the story of Sharon's illness, is a story of faith and the mystical power of the Forty-Sixth Psalm, which provided comfort to a woman helpless to hold back the tide of approaching death, but who replied—three weeks shy of her passing—to a healthcare worker wondering how she could still smile, "I'm not alone, ever."

And then she whispered, with a small smile, "If I didn't have Jesus Christ in my heart I'd be scared to death. But he is here and I am not scared. I am *okay*."

Psalm 46, she whispered to the young woman, "Ps 46, God's word, provides so much strength. I am *okay*."

That is faith. And this is largely the account of the spiritual life of a selfless woman of faith who was determined to smile in the face of death, to care about those around her even as she progressively lost control of her body, and maintained a calm that affected medical staff and visitors alike. Those caring for her, those visiting, left her bedside inexplicably hopeful for their own futures. Faith can often be contagious.

I overheard the brief conversation of one couple as they left her room in our home:

"I don't know why, but I feel so much more thankful and encouraged about our lives. Usually, I dread these kinds of visits but now I feel . . ." He hesitated, searching for the word.

"Hopeful?" she supplied.

He thought for a moment, then his serious face slid into a smile. "Yes, and even joyful. Certainly, as she said, 'okay.'"

The last words I heard him say as they went out the door: "Let's take a look at Ps 46."

The Spirit of "Okay"

It is a testament to the spiritual effects of God's word, the Bible, and therein her singular touchstone, Ps 46, which she pulled from the Old Testament and committed to memory. The psalm was her all, eleven verses that she haltingly puzzled out after the childhood trauma of sexual abuse, and then enthusiastically embraced throughout her life. She spent her last weeks communicating its power in the hope that her family would achieve the same ability to meet the challenges of life by unleashing the spiritual power of God through Ps 46.

"Be still and know that I am God" was a profane taunt of her abuser. But, in Spirit-driven irony, the mystical holiness of "Be still and know that I am God" and its surrounding Ps 46 became an integral part of a simple yet amazingly powerful and lifelong faith that celebrated the joy of being one of God's created creatures despite, as she called it, the *stinkin' stuff* of life. It helped her live—strong and positive and thankful—the ordinary, often extraordinary challenges encountered in this world.

So, let's unpack her *okay*:

Okay means I'm suffering but suffering is not who I am; I am about life and hope . . . right up until I draw my last breath.

Okay means I love my family, my relationships, and the life with which I've been blessed . . . right up until I draw my last breath.

Okay means I can communicate and encourage others, despite the trauma of illness and tragic experiences, to help them link to the Spirit of God and thereby find joy in the simple living of life . . . right up until I draw my last breath.

Okay means I'll bear the burden of my illness in such a way as to demonstrate the power of my faith, itself a possibly painful form of Christian, of Godly witness . . . right up until I draw my last breath.

Okay means that I know—I mean rock solid, way down deep *know* despite occasional uncertainty and doubt—that my life will never end, that heaven and Jesus will welcome me with open arms, and that I will ultimately stand healed before God, the ravages of this terrible disease forgotten . . . and I will know this right up until I draw my last breath.

Okay means that, once I've drawn that last breath, it's a whole new ballgame, that I'll live the "thank you Jesus" that has kept me going through the *stinkin' stuff* of life.

She was confident that, with some coaching, I would share her certainty that life would never end and faith would guide me through grief to a joyful life—again, in the here and now. By the final morning of her illness, when ALS had destroyed the muscles in her lungs and she took her last breath, I had faithfully prayed through, as she asked, the calming power of Ps 46.

Her death caused pain, yes. But I knew that heaven and Jesus had welcomed her with open arms, where and before whom she stood healed, the ravages of Lou Gehrig's Disease forgotten, and the scars from the other *stinkin' stuff* in her life left behind. I took to heart our conversations and—as instructed—worked through my grief and developed empowering faith and encouragement and resilience, and an understanding of God's love and promises.

The Inspiration of Psalm 46

I began writing this book during the last six weeks of her life, while sitting beside her bed and waiting for her to wake up and continue our conversations, her "lessons" as she called them. Each evening and, when up to it, at various times throughout the night, she communicated intensity of love and purpose, determined to change the rest of my life—the life I would live without her.

Those lessons revolved around Ps 46, written by the sons of Korah back in the thirteenth century before Christ. The sons of Korah had experienced the loss of their ancient ancestor and other members of his household when the first Korah had led a large-scale revolt against Moses and his sponsor (God) during the exodus from Egypt. Urged on by his wife and assorted sycophants, Korah attempted to seize power and establish an Israelite kingdom driven by a lust for privilege, and conformity to the barbaric practices of the peoples surrounding them in the ancient Middle East. There was little doubt that such an approach would soon degenerate into the idol-worshipping and depraved sacrificial cultures that were the norm of the era. But God would have none of it: he quickly dispatched Korah and his thousands of followers to an agonizing death.

However, the House of Korah—a generational line also known as the sons of Korah—continued on, with each successive generation demonstrating its rectitude and service until, finally, the sons of Korah were promoted, and became the Sons of Korah. The Korahite tribes were admired by others in the fledgling Israelite nation for their ability to put ancestral tragedy aside and produce commanding worship music centered on the power of God, faith, and spiritual connection. The patriarch Korah? Ptooey! Wish it weren't so, but he rebelled in the name of power and personal aggrandizement, and God stopped him before the Israelite nation could become just another brutal child-sacrificing, women-raping, horror-filled hell on earth.

The Sons of Korah had faith, and became admired popular musicians and worship song writers in the new nation of Israel. Among the worship poems they created and put to music was Ps 46, a tribute to the joy-enabling power of God who gets us through the turmoil and troubles of this world:

> 1 God is our refuge and strength,
>   always ready to help in times of trouble.
> 2 So we will not fear when earthquakes come
>   and the mountains crumble into the sea.
> 3 Let the oceans roar and foam.
>   Let the mountains tremble as the waters surge!
> 4 A river brings joy to the city of our God,
>   the sacred home of the Most High.
> 5 God dwells in that city; it cannot be destroyed.
>   From the very break of day, God will protect it.
> 6 The nations are in chaos,
>   and their kingdoms crumble!
>   God's voice thunders,
>   and the earth melts!
> 7 The Lord of Heaven's Armies is here among us;
>   the God of Israel is our fortress. *Interlude*
> 8 Come, see the glorious works of the Lord:
>   See how he brings destruction upon the world.
> 9 He causes wars to end throughout the earth.
>   He breaks the bow and snaps the spear;
>   he burns the shields with fire.
> 10 "Be still, and know that I am God!
>   I will be honored by every nation.
>   I will be honored throughout the world."
> 11 The Lord of Heaven's Armies is here among us;
>   the God of Israel is our fortress.

How Soon We Forget

Sharon's lessons, drawn in love and faith and wisdom from Ps 46, were designed to provide her family with a happy and healthy life following her death, despite the grief that she knew would threaten to take up permanent residence in our household. As promised, I followed her prescription for overcoming that devastating sorrow, and was soon living a normal and fulfilled life . . . just as she had intended.

And then . . . I forgot. So normal, so fulfilled . . . I forgot. Her passing, her lessons of her last six weeks—indeed, her life—faded into a bittersweet but distant memory, as did my work on this book. I remarried, one of my two daughters had my first grand-child, followed by a second, while the other settled into a career, and life was good; "very good," to borrow the description in the Genesis creation story when "God looked over all he had made, and he saw that it was very good!"

But then came the unexpected, resurrecting memories of my late wife's ALS diagnosis of disease, with the pronouncement by an oncologist at the cancer center in Lynchburg, Virginia that I had Stage 4 Hodgkin's Lymphoma. Hodgkin's is a blood disease that quickly destroys the germ-fighting system of the body. Over the next year, as my immune system was compromised, this cancer morphed into a particular virulent form of blood disease that resisted all combinations of chemotherapy.

"There's nothing more we can do for you here," the oncologist sadly told me and my new wife, Victoria. Best chance to live: a stem cell transplant. So off we went, seventy-five miles, to tap the expertise of the University of Virginia (UVA) cancer center, where after years of treatment I remain a patient.

Stem cell transplants are extraordinarily painful, but can be extremely effective, especially given the expertise available at UVA. For chemotherapy-resistant Hodgkin's Lymphoma sufferers, they are a treatment of the last resort. All the stem cells—bone marrow and white blood cells—of the patient are eradicated, which destroys the immune system in the process. I underwent two types of stem cell transplants, as the cancer proved distressingly stubborn. In addition, my compromised immune system opened me to everything from pneumonia to graft-versus-host disease (GVHD), which attacked my muscles, at one point leaving me unable to walk or lift my arms. But the expertise of the medical specialists and other healthcare staff brought me back. For that I thank the University of Virginia and God, not necessarily in that order.

Long nights in hospital rooms, in hotels, and furnished apartments from which I would return each day for infusions of blood, platelets and pain killers. Chemotherapy that destroyed the cancer cells and existing blood cells, but sometimes left me in my room in the hospital, my eyes closed and praying that I could make it through.

During all this my new wife, Victoria, was extraordinary, taking care of me in what quickly became a full-time caregiving job. My health had forced me into retirement, having been robbed of the mental acuity and physical ability to continue working. Looking back on it, I was blessed by an army of skilled healthcare professionals, both in Lynchburg (our home) and at UVA, and a determined wife whose devotion was awe-inspiring. But there were times when it seemed like the curses far outweighed the blessings; such is life with disease. Up and down, swings of mood, drifting from illness-driven crisis to crisis.

Psalm 46 as a Lifesaver

Two steps forward and three steps back, or so it seemed. My muscles, lungs, liver, almost every major organ in my body were invaded by the cancer cells. The treatments were excruciatingly painful. After more than four years of cancer, three years of fighting, I was exhausted. My biggest fear had come to pass: I had hit a wall, both physically and emotionally. My soul ached with the thought that I would be unable give Victoria a husband and friend with whom to once again walk and live and love with some degree of normalcy.

Victoria stood firm, stubbornly firm. You can do it, she encouraged, I'll help. You can do it. I know you can. But behind a veil of pain, a voice whispered, at times screamed, "I can't. I can't!"

Then, during one particularly painful treatment that had me collapsed on the floor, my muscles refusing to move, eyes tearing, and silently begging God for mercy, my mind went back more than eight years to the ordeal of my late wife as she battled ALS. Her extraordinary faith in God, her personal connection to the Spirit, her beyond-natural strength during that last year before her death was astounding. And her faith and joy during those last six weeks before she died were nothing short of miraculous . . . and inspiring.

My promise to her . . . remembered.

Her lessons . . . rushing back.

And hope . . . resurrected.

Yes, Said Sharon, There *Is* a Way to Draw Strength from God

During those weeks, she ignored the pain of her slowly dying muscles, refused to think about the coming and inevitable closing down of her breathing, and helped me understand her almost supernatural perseverance and cheer. Faith, connection, and especially that psalm's tenth verse, "Be still, and know that I am God," was the gateway to beyond-natural perseverance and ability to overcome. She pointed to the whole of Ps 46 as both a starting and ending point that would get me through the grief of her passing, my wife and best friend of almost thirty-three years, and continue with my life.

"Psalm 46," she said softly, haltingly. "Ps 46, the words of God and gateway to his Spirit, his strength, will always be there for you, regardless of how difficult the challenge, whatever you face." And so her purpose-driven "lessons" came cascading back. Psalm 46, I remembered with my face pressed against the hospital floor, was the secret sauce. Her words.

I had been astonished to discover, as her death neared, that it had been her "go-to" since the age of seven, and had helped her overcome the challenges, many minor but a few horrific, that she faced over the years. And when confronted with the *"stinkin' stuff"* of life, as she put it, her invariable response was to *"Ps-46 it."*

At that time, I listened to her closely, and memorized and applied Ps 46, first because she asked, and then because it worked.

It got me through grief as few other parts of the Bible had; it strengthened my faith; and offered perseverance and hope. However, the memories—although not the lessons—faded as the good times again began to roll. I remarried; one of my daughters had my first grandchildren, girls, while the other settled into a career; and life was both good and normal, with the usual minor, everyday challenges.

But now, disaster. A virulent form of cancer. And Sharon and Ps 46 came rushing back. At one point, pain put me on the floor in the hospital. It was then that a memory flashed of her approach to tragedy and challenge to me, to use the psalm, beginning with its tenth verse, as the gateway to spiritual support, love, and perseverance. Verse 10.

I stopped struggling with an uncooperative body and rested my head on the cold, tiled floor. "Be still and know that I am God!" Verse 10 done right, an opening to the supernatural, beyond-natural universe of God, and a personal connection to his Spirit. Let your mind run through the psalm in its entirety once you've established and breathed the stillness, she had said. After I had been helped to my bed, Victoria later—carefully avoiding the ever-present intravenous lines—handed me a Bible.

Behold the Magic

The psalm was long forgotten, driven out of my mind by a normal life, good times, the fog of chemotherapy and other drugs. But its magic was still there, in the book of Psalms, and in the determined lessons of the last six weeks of the life of my late wife.

To paraphrase the most memorable line from any newspaper of all time—apart from the wisdom of the Ten Commandments —written at the end of the nineteenth century: Yes, Virginia, there is a God . . . and he emanates from the eleven verses of poetry comprising Ps 46.

2

A Doctor Speaks,
a Body Speaks, God Speaks

In Which a Dying Woman of Faith Smiles and Loves

SHE DID AS SHE always did: Smile.

But this time it was in the face of a terminal disease. Smile, as she always had, despite the setbacks and roadblocks, the oft-searing stuff that life had thrown and was throwing at her now in a neurologist's office at the University of Virginia Health Center. Months of testing with the following result: You have ALS, amyotrophic lateral sclerosis, popularly known as Lou Gehrig's Disease. The disease is terminal and, in your case, progressing rapidly. A devastating diagnosis, and then, in reaction . . . stillness, tears, and inevitably, a smile.

That smile reflected the joy in her soul, her endless faith that all would work out in the end, "courtesy of God, his voice amplified through the stillness," she pronounced softly later as we waited for our car to be brought from the hospital valet parking.

Yes, she really talked like that; faith was never far from the surface. After the diagnosis, after the tears, we stood outside the medical buildings in the damp December cold at her insistence, waiting for our car. The lobby was warm, but she insisted on being outside.

"I want to feel the weather," she said, savoring the bite of the wind. "I want to feel everything this coming year, appreciate God's grace. And I want to have many, many conversations with Jesus." She chuckled. "I'm getting a bit poetical, aren't I?"

I looked at her. I had gotten used to Sharon by now, almost thirty-five years after we had met, more than thirty years of marriage. She loved life, she loved to love, and she loved God, and all his facets: Father, Son, and Holy Spirit. She loved the One God, who supplied strength through trauma and tribulation, gave her strength now, and would give her strength as the disease progressed. God had walked her through life, blessed her . . . and now he would walk her through this illness, to a new beginning. This she believed with all her heart.

Even now, when the normal of our life together had come to a screeching halt in the hospital buildings behind us. The neurologists at the University of Virginia medical center summarized their testing, done after two years of decline that had mystified the doctors in our Virginia hometown seventy-five miles to the southwest.

We had sat for hours as neurologists and staff sympathetically explained: The disease causes the sufferer to rapidly lose control of the muscles that govern critical body functions such as breathing and movement. The nerves that connect the brain to the muscles controlling every square inch of the body die, with the result that the muscles controlling the body's voluntary functions quickly atrophy, one after another. ALS, for which there is no cure or treatment to significantly extend life, sentences the sufferer to a slow, inexorable death, anywhere from two to five years on the average after the formal diagnosis.

Kick in the Head, Stab Through the Heart

"Are you okay?" she asked as we waited for the car.

I shook my head, still amazed at how she looked at the world.

"*You're* asking *me* that? I'm worried about you—this is not just a kick in the head, it's a stab through the heart. And you're worried about me?" I took a deep breath, thinking of the disease the doctors and staff had laid out for us.

Bottom line: Each day would be worse than the next, as the complex brain cells would no longer direct the movement of the millions of muscles that animate the body. ALS is a death sentence: walking . . . gone; finger movement . . . gone; swallowing . . . gone; breathing . . . gone; digestion, eye movement, chewing, all of the bodily functions that we take for granted, all directed by networks of muscles . . . gone. Suffering and death: Guaranteed.

As one doctor said sorrowfully to me in an aside outside the examining room that the disease is "as bad as it gets" when it comes to suffering and despair.

How long did she have left on this earth? Certainly, the disease is progressing rapidly, but it's hard to say. We're so close to a cure; why, a cure might even happen in the next few months. Or in the next year or so. All of which are true: The ALS Society, UVA, other hospitals, and research facilities have this and other neuromuscular diseases on their research radar.

"How long?"

"Well, some people go on for years, decades even. And what with our clinics, our expert staff, our expert neurologists . . . It's hard to say. You never know."

Three to five years, maybe more. "You never know."

Psalm-46 It: The Beast in My Body

But later, outside the hospital, Sharon had a different take than the doctors and assorted healthcare professionals who had examined her. She knew.

"'You never know'?" she repeated. And then she said plaintively, "I know. I know. It's coming fast, the beast in my body."

"The beast in your body?"

"The beast in my body," she confirmed quietly, standing at my side, watching the cars and ambulances crawling in front of

13

the hospital. That's what she called it, "the beast in her body," an alien and evil presence of a disease that would radically shorten and alter the remainder of our lives together. Our world had been turned upside down; trite, but true.

"I don't have two to five years. I have one year, maybe fourteen months at the most. I can feel it, I can just feel it."

She turned, put her arms around my neck and held tight, sobbing quietly into my ear. "I don't want to leave you alone. I don't want to leave you alone. I don't want to leave you alone."

We stood in silence, arms encircling each other, there in front of the hospital with the end of the day coming fast, the gray of the early winter dusk enveloping us. And then, in the cold, after holding each other for what seemed an eternity, she drew back, wiped her eyes, and smiled sadly, "Well, we have a lot of work to do. I have to get you ready for life after me. I have somewhere around a year left."

"How do you know? They said . . ."

"I know what they said, that I may have years," she replied. "But I know, I just *feel* what's ahead. They can test, they can diagnose, they can poke and prod; but I can feel it inside, feel this thing eating at me. There is so much I need to tell you, to talk about, to fit in the year ahead, to prepare you."

"Prepare *me*?"

"Prepare *you*," she said gently. "Get you ready for life . . ." She hesitated, then continued, ". . . after I'm gone."

"Can't get there from here," I murmured, shaking my head.

"You can and will," she said. "You'll learn to *Ps-46 it*."

"Psalm 46?" I repeated quizzically.

"*Psalm-46 it*, a verb," she said. "You'll use Ps 46 the way God intended all of his word to be used, his Spirit '*always ready to help in times of trouble*,' his love and support magnified because '*the Lord of Heaven's Armies is here among us; the God of Israel is our fortress*.'" She leaned her head against my chest, looking at the concrete walk.

I relaxed my arms and stepped back, but still holding her. "God stuff, huh? And never-imagined *stinkin' stuff*. But I'll do it, I'll learn. If it's important to you, right here and right now, a promise—I will learn."

She smiled. A teary-eyed smile, but still a smile. "*Stinkin' stuff*, yes," she sniffed.

No Black Despair

Stinkin' stuff had become part of family lore when our daughters, Brittany and Chelsea, then very young and now grown and on their own, would say when encountering a challenging situation, "That's really '*stinkin' stuff*." We had quickly picked up the term, using it to describe unhappy and, at times, heartbreaking circumstances and occurrences. Every relationship, every marriage has them.

"Psalm 46," she sighed. "I thought I'd wait until we're together more after retirement to discuss how it's guided my life. You know, talk while traveling. Our idyll, a hotel balcony overlooking the ocean, glasses of sweet tea in our hands. Hair gray—if you would have any left," she chuckled—"watching the waves gently caressing the sand."

"The whole travel brochure, retirement," I added with a sad smile. "No work, just the two of us."

"It seems it's not going to happen," she said. "Those waves aren't caressing; they're crashing on the sand. So, now, I need to give you a foundation for working through grief and living well. That will be my legacy for you and through you, the girls. A good life, a Spirit-guided life. A joyful life; despite my illness, despite my passing, despite your grief. You, and through you, the girls, going on. Living."

For Sharon, no whining, no screaming, no looking back in black despair. Standing outside the hospital, waiting for the car, she explained: "The future—not the one we expected and planned for. Now I have to look into a future that we won't have together, and give the gift of God, easily digested advice and mentoring." Her mission: She wanted to leave hope, to enable her family to carry on despite her pain and passing, and our hurt as we participated—our daughters from a distance with occasional visits, me by her side, always, as her caregiver—in her inevitable decline.

"My death is a 'given,'" she said flatly. "Of course, I hope not, I pray not; but absent a last-minute reprieve, there's only have enough time to prepare you for life after me.'"

"After," I sighed.

"Yes, after me," she nodded, an introspective smile on her face.

As American as Apple Pie

I looked as she stood against the gray windows of the medical center, shivering in the cold wind and the aftermath of the diagnosis. She was extraordinary, this ordinary woman from a southern mountain state, emblematic of the solid faith and values of most of the women who make up this nation. They work, raise their families, play, worship and pray, give their all to relationships, and live a life largely unaffected by the cascade of noise emanating from the trendy enclaves of the east and west coasts, from social media; from the universities, from the do-anything-for-power centers of the nation, and the arrogance of the self-appointed arbiters of the behaviors and values of the rest of us. These are women who stand on the rock of faith, commitment, and family values. The *real* feminists. You see them in church, in synagogue, at picnics and state fairs, content in the belief that faith can overcome what our young daughters labeled the *stinkin' stuff*, that faith allows them to simply live their lives.

Sharon was not a celebrity, a professional athlete, a media news star, a politician snorting like a racehorse in the starting gate at the sight of a television news crew. She rarely posted on Facebook, didn't use Twitter or Instagram, never had a video go viral on YouTube—nor were those her desires.

Her primary job was to raise her children, taking to heart the biblical disciplines of demonstrating restraint and commitment, teaching values by example, and doing what was right. As she told a senior executive from the hotel chain where she had worked in marketing, visiting in our Atlanta home after the birth of our first daughter, "I want to raise her right, instill the right values, and have her understand that she may choose any direction she wishes, as long as she lives with honor and purpose."

The senior executive looked at her, at the newborn in her arms, and said, "Sweetie, you could have had it all. But a full-time mom?"

Sharon smiled, a soft and shining smile. "I *do* have it all," she whispered. "And so will this girl, as long as she learns 'to act justly and to love mercy and to walk humbly,' whatever her path."

The executive raised her eyebrows.

Sharon chuckled quietly. "God stuff," she explained . . . with a smile. Sharon had as many types of smiles as an Eskimo has words for snow.

In her own words, "I'm ordinary," a girl from rural West Virginia who had reserves of strength and love and perseverance, all of which she had demonstrated throughout her life . . . and protracted death.

Ordinary, yes, but heroically so in a way that all the publicity seekers, the me-me-me's jostling each other for a media spotlight, have never been nor will ever be. She possessed the strength and courage of an ordinary woman anchored by faith and love, turning ordinary into extraordinary and allowing her to calmly face a tragically truncated future.

In her faith, her ability to overcome, to persevere, and in her strength and common sense: As American as apple pie.

Poverty, Rape, Abuse, Discrimination: Be Still . . .

That was then, and this is now.

"Another bump on the road," she sighed.

I looked at her as I forced a ghost of a smile. Bumps on the road? Many, and at times, sinkholes, and washed-out bridges. To me, this was all of that combined, and then some. An unimaginable chasm. But for Sharon, as I came to understand in those last six weeks of her life, a terminal disease was simply one more challenge, albeit her last.

She had experienced poverty as the only child of a single mother in rural West Virginia; faux-Christian intolerance and bullying ("I was threatened with hell just about every day in childcare"); sexual abuse as a little girl in that same childcare situation; and government schools that insisted upon lowered horizons for female graduates, discouraging them from aspiring to jobs other than, say, secretary or hotel maid.

In her late teens, she wandered into an emotionally abusive first marriage; began her twenties being raped at knifepoint; experienced the resulting trauma of abortion and years of regret for the child she never met. Later, when she left a promising career in public relations to marry and have children, she endured mockery from women who disapproved of her choice of family over career; who ridiculed her insistence that motherhood is, indeed, a career; and who let her know—in those decades of intolerant and arrogant feminism, a precursor to today's "woke" madness—that centering her life on children and family is archaic, a "form of slavery," they howled.

The Calming Power of God Stuff

But Sharon went her own way, tasting God's spiritual connection and smiles and coping skills that come from drawing strength and wisdom from the tranquility and connected-ness of faith ("Be still and know . . .") that leads to supernatural, spiritual strength and discernment (". . . and know that I am God").

How can you not be bitter?

"I have to now work at not being bitter, on being there for you and those around me. With the help of the Spirit—who also leads me to so many other, appropriate parts of God's word—I won't melt, like the Wicked Witch of the West into a puddle of something nasty and unpleasant on the floor."

During the coming year, she would experience pain and suffering; ALS, indeed any chronic or terminal disease, is not for the faint of heart. Cancer, heart disease, muscle disorders, etc., so many incurable and ongoing diseases that affect more than 40 percent of the country; all take their toll, both physically and emotionally. And now Sharon had joined the five persons out of 100,000 with ALS. Statistically, less than the chance of winning some lotteries, a miniscule percentage.

But here we stood. The diagnosis was conclusive. She had it. But she also had faith and, as a result, hope for a better future, with that same hope for her family. Faith that in the now and the great unknown after her passing, God would take care of her. Faith that her at first practiced and now innate stillness arising out of Ps 46 would give her the wisdom and strength in the time she had left to guide her family, through me, to living well and joyfully after the trauma of her passing.

What differentiated between Sharon and the vast majority of ALS patients? What allowed her to smile even as her health declined?

Faith. Faith, pure and simple. Unconditional faith.

"'Be still and know that I am God,'" she murmured, there on the sidewalk in the cold and gray of both the winter weather and her diagnosis. "The Spirit of God will help us through this, despite knowing what's ahead."

Then she recited Ps 46 from memory, clutching at my arm.

When finished, she stood motionless. I looked at her quizzically.

"You're wondering why I'm reciting that psalm," she said. "This whole thing, the diagnosis, is so hard to wrap my head around. And when something is this hard, this terrible, my mind goes to Psalm 46. Since I was a little girl. The psalm is poetry and allegory and metaphor, promises and literal descriptions, and above all it's personal. Layer upon layer of meaning and personal assurance. I want you to remember this, the verse that taps into my heart. It is my connecting soul, and will eventually tap into your heart and kick off your personal relationship with the Spirit . . . if you listen."

She closed her eyes and recited: "'Be still, and know that I am God!'"

"Bible stuff," I whispered weakly.

"Yes, God stuff," she nodded, taking a deep breath followed by a smile, a tender and comforting smile that understood and accepted the diagnosis. Another type of smile, another type of snow.

Despair? Desolation? *Psalm-46 it* for Hope!

I weakly repeated. "Bible stuff, huh?"

"God stuff," she said. "The equal, and then some, of *stinkin' stuff.*"

She smiled again, a soft smile that somehow cut through the gathering gloom at the end of the day, a gentle smile that reached out and reassured, and at the same time turned inward, drawing on that sense of calm that she had always, regardless of circumstance, and had now, notwithstanding the extraordinarily *stinkin' stuff* we faced.

Sharon did not fall to pieces, as so many have in the face of medical challenges. She didn't descend into the black despair of depression, living out the remainder of her days angry and miserable and drugged out on the many coping medicines offered by her healthcare providers.

Why? Because *"stuff* happens, *stinkin' stuff* even," she said and, once she had accepted the news, explained where I would need to go from here. "And I have faith and the certainty that God is with me, always."

"*Psalm-46 it,*" she said quietly, and then nodded. "*Psalm-46 it.* That's what I have left to explain to you and, through you, the girls. We'll start with just a bit of travel, and then finish at the house. Most of what I have to say will take us through our last two months together."

I looked at her, puzzled.

Bam Went the Gavel! Death Came the Verdict. But Happy Ending? You Bet!!

"It seems grim now," she said. "But we'll adjust, find our way through the next year."

"You really think so?"

"Yes, I do, love, you *will* adjust. With my help, with renewed faith and a growing confidence in God." She'd had much time to think about it during those hours in the neurology offices, she explained. In fact, she'd been thinking about it in all the previous months of testing, during the eighty-minute drives back and forth to the testing at the UVA Health Center in Charlottesville, Virginia and in the previous year as her muscles inexplicably twitched and her gait became labored.

What if, what if, what if . . . something was seriously wrong? Something that put her on the path to a wheelchair—or worse. What if she became seriously ill? Now, finally, the tests had presented their case, the doctors had assessed the results, and our wait for the certainty of a diagnosis was at an end.

And it hit: *Bam!* went the gavel; *Death!* came the verdict.

Hope, With or Without a Cure

Now we knew: She was going to die, and it was to be a painful death. She would suffer during the year ahead, especially near the end, guaranteed. Sixty years on this earth, more than three decades of marriage, our plans for enjoying each other without the distractions of the outside world of careers and bustle, for watching two daughters at the beginnings of their careers and marriages—only one marriage at the time, as our younger daughter was engaged when we were slammed with Sharon's diagnosis—and grandchildren, and had come to a screeching halt.

That was the bottom line. Our daughters were devastated. I was shocked. But Sharon remained Sharon and, after her initial tears, did what she had done for all of her life: accept reality and continue walking, smiling even; smiling, especially.

The doctors, the ALS neurology staff had tried to balance the news, provide reasons for optimism. "There's a lot of research going on," one said. "We may wake up one day and find that they have a cure. There's hope." True enough, but the pace of neurological breakthroughs is slow while ALS progresses rapidly.

Sharon smiled through the tears; she was only human after all. She surprised the neurologists, her reaction unexpected.

"No matter, there's hope, with or without a cure," she told them, sitting on the examining table. "I have hope because I have faith. And while I will pray for a cure, I'm not counting on it. My focus will be on my family, who I will prepare for the future. And I'll do that through my husband," she said, nodding to me.

The neurologist and his staff stood in silence, not knowing quite what to say. Hysteria they understood. Anger. Uncontrollable tears. Denial. Depression. Those walls, those examining rooms, had seen so much of that. But faith? Not so much. And smiles? They were perplexed. You could see it on their faces. Is she living in an alternate universe? Did she not understand, she had Lou Gehrig's Disease? That she would suffer? That she would experience a painful death, suffocation followed by heart failure?

Ah, such a strange creature, this woman of faith. Shock, we understand; denial, we understand. But acceptance and faith? Insanity!

I walked outside, pushing her wheelchair, and then helped her out of it. We stood together, waiting for our car. Then she spoke.

"They're good people, talented medical people," she said, watching the street. "But they don't understand how faith, how belief in God, in Jesus will get me through the year ahead. They've offered a diagnosis followed by treatments that will ease the pain . . . somewhat. But I have to consider your pain, you, and the girls. Through God's grace, that consideration lessens my pain."

I rubbed my eyes with open palms, then sighed deeply.

She nodded, standing still, hand looped through my arm. "And they don't understand my job, which will be to give you a happy ending. Not *the* happy ending, the one we've planned; but *a* happy ending, the one that God is helping us with, the one that prepares you for life without me, without the future we've envisioned. Different ending for all of us."

Another sigh. Heavy sigh, accompanied by tears. My tears.

"And that ending begins with the tenth verse of Ps 46, 'Be still and know that I am God!' In that stillness you—we—will find an answer to getting through this . . . and coming out happy and at peace. Both of us."

I said nothing.

A Guide to Conquering Grief

"Family, friends—do some visiting. That will take a bit more than ten months. Then we'll cap our journeys off with a couple of months or so of good hard talk, before I lose my speech." She glanced over at me from the passenger seat. "I love you. You'll get through this; I'll get through this. Looking ahead to the lessons are important, it gives me purpose . . . and assurance that I've done all that's possible for you to live joyfully and, through you, the girls after I'm gone."

"Gone," I repeated, staring with unseeing eyes at the ambulances in the street.

Looking back, it's easy to see what she had in mind: Conquer grief; tamp down despair; live a good life, a fulfilled life and, especially, a Spirit-driven life . . . after her passing.

Lessons delivered; Lessons received. Her brief remaining life, my life then and now, our lives together, were all the better for it. Her legacy of love and faith.

The valet brought the car, and we began the seventy-five-mile drive home. Our journey had begun in the light, but was ending in the dark. We were living now a metaphor of gloom, I thought as we navigated the busy pedestrian crosswalks on the road between the hospital buildings, and it felt . . . awful, just awful.

I glanced over at her in the passenger seat.

She wiped away the tears, turned, and smiled.

"We must have faith that all things will work together for good in our lives. God guarantees it."

"Bible stuff," I said flatly.

"Yes, the New Testament, Romans . . . and, as with the Old Testament, God stuff . . . really good God stuff. It—He—is all the same. What is it your grandma used to pray? *'Shema Yisrael, Adonai Elohenu, Adonai echad.'* 'Listen, O Israel! The Lord is our God, the Lord alone. And you must love the Lord your God with all your heart, all your soul, and all your strength.' Both a prescription and a challenge."

"A challenge?"

"To get out of our minds, to tap into his resources, to allow him to help. Through faith."

"You spent a lot of time with her," I commented.

"Yes," she said. "We've got a hard road ahead, but it's reassuring we'll have him and all of his power with us every step of the way."

An awesome woman . . . of faith.

3

Faith and Donuts

Fast Forward Ten Months

TEN MONTHS PASSED QUICKLY between the diagnosis and the "beginning of the beginning, for both of us," as Sharon characterized our last six weeks ("give or take a few weeks," she said).

"My passing is inevitable—there's nothing we can do about it. Mourn, certainly, but also look on it as an opportunity for you and the girls to draw closer to each other, and to infuse your lives with the Spirit of God. Why? Because you'll turn debilitating grief into manageable grief, be happier and make better decisions. And your thoughts of me will be filled with joyful remembrances, rather than sad emptiness."

We had settled back into our southwestern Virginia home after drives to view and, as Sharon put it, feel the ocean in Nova Scotia, Virginia and Myrtle beaches, and Hilton Head Island. In Nova Scotia we drove the seaside highway circling Cape Breton, where she watched the whales gamboling and breathed the chilly, bracing air of that Atlantic Ocean province of Canada. In addition, we visited many of the shops of the crafters, glass blowers and sculptors who, over the years, have made that pristine Canadian island an artist's colony, and whose works Sharon had periodically purchased in art galleries.

Our short trips were punctuated by many visits to the ALS clinic at the University of Virginia (UVA), where they tracked the progress of the disease and offered what small relief they could; a feeding tube, for example, was put in her stomach when—during the early summer trip to Nova Scotia—she lost the ability to chew and swallow her food, although she could still speak; a visit with a pulmonologist for medicine that deadened the pain of her struggling to draw a breath in the humidity of the southern summer; and prescriptions for oxygen and other medical devices that would assist in breathing and somewhat—only somewhat, because ALS inevitably forces fluid to collect in the lungs—bring relief.

In early fall, the doctors judged the disease progressing faster than they had originally diagnosed, although not faster than Sharon—who was intimately acquainted with "the beast in my body" that told her time was running out—thought, although you "never know what tomorrow will bring" in the way of a medical breakthrough. Sharon, now bound to a wheelchair, then pronounced us ready to begin intensive mentoring, the goal of which was to reshape my instincts and provide me with the ability to "not just survive, but thrive after I'm . . ."

I knew what was expected of me by that time: ". . . gone," I finished.

"My gut, feeding tube and all, is telling me that I have only a few months left at most, despite the encouraging words of the staff at the ALS clinic. I appreciate their reassurance and it certainly makes the visits to Charlottesville less depressing," she said. "But all the nice words in the world can't get around the fact there's no known cure for ALS and it's progressing rapidly in me."

"*Yet*," I emphasized, unable to let go of the last shards of hope for a medical miracle, and then echoed the words we heard on each visit to the clinic. "'No known cure *yet*,' they say—but you never know, a breakthrough may come soon, this week even." For me, the year since the diagnosis had been filled, dueling-banjo style, with "a breakthrough may come soon" of the ALS clinic and Sharon's "after I die." And, of course, her smiles. So many of them, tinged with a variety of emotions. Maybe a bit sadder at times, but still smiles. Those pesky Eskimos and their nuanced gradations of snow combined with the Christmas classic of Frank Sinatra in my head: Let it snow! Let it snow! Let it snow!

"Someday there will be," she replied. "But it will be too late for us. So, let's get busy with you, with preparing you. It gives us a purpose, and a purpose will keep us from dwelling on what's happening."

Preparations

Shortly, it had become increasingly difficult for her to use our main bedroom. We had already made the decision for her to remain at home rather than undergo institutionalized hospice care in a setting that, no matter how dressed up with art on the walls, was basically a hospital room. I worked out a weekly schedule with the hospice nurses and aides to visit, hired part-time aides and arranged to work part-time. I regularly drove home during the day to check on her progress and, understanding her modesty, assist with her personal dressing, grooming and toilette activities. The latter was made easier by remodeling a bathroom to fit her needs.

No longer able to move her legs without support, and with her arms becoming increasingly weak, I moved the furniture from the guest room, situated across the hall from the master bedroom, and equipped it for taking care of her. Adaptive bed assistance products made her as comfortable as possible in the house, devices to help clear her mouth and throat, breathe and communicate. ALS organizations were extremely helpful in outfitting her room.

At her suggestion, I purchased a classic front desk bell that she could tap by moving a finger, and put a remote-control device within easy reach for the lights in both of our rooms. She used these to alert me to her needs, turning on the lights in various parts of the house—especially the master bedroom, where I still slept—with a touch of the finger. This, with the bell, would ensure that I would quickly jump out of bed or hurry from another area of the house, grab the wheelchair, and roll her to the remodeled bathroom. Her bedroom was outfitted with bedside credenzas and multiple glass shelves that allowed easy access to medical devices for both me and the technicians that serviced them. Tablets and books were always placed within easy reach of hands and fingers that were steadily losing the ability to move.

Funeral, Coffin, Cemetery

At her insistence, we made funeral arrangements, choosing a coffin and selecting a cemetery. Her strength, her grounding in reality, her emphasis on the well-being of her family and lack of self-pity astounded those who visited and those who helped care for her.

"I don't want you to be anxious about these things," she said. "My final weeks are for me and you, two people in love, two great friends just talking about the future of one of them. And, as much as possible, the girls."

"So much to think about," I said sadly.

"Lose the long face," she rasped. "This will leave time for us to set you on the right path."

"I don't know how you do it, sweetheart." I shook my head once again, sighing deeply.

"Be still," she replied, "and find peace. Psalm 46: 'God's voice thunders, and the earth melts!' A very personal part of that earth is my fear, the ever-threatening bitterness. Not easy, but I've had a lot of practice over a lifetime. More than you know."

"More than I know?"

"More than you know," she repeated. "I'll tell you about some of it, but only to affirm the need for you to walk in harmony with Ps 46, verse 10, and wherever else it leads you in God's word. I know I sound weird, insisting on that now, spending our last weeks together talking about something that we've rarely talked about during our years together. But I want the grief you'll have to be healthy, not burden you in the years to come. Promise to grieve and cry healthy."

I shook my head, not in denial but in wonder. Again.

Goldilocks and the Three Bears

At the funeral home I wheeled her from casket to casket as she contemplated her final resting place. She chose a stained and polished oak casket.

"Goldilocks and the three bears," she said as we waited to finish the arrangements. "One of the bears in a wheelchair. Not too expensive, not too simple; but just right. Now you don't have to think about this; instead, we'll spend our time talking and just being together." She also had me drive her to all the cemeteries in the area, and picked a site on a hill in a rural cemetery with the Blue Ridge Mountains in the distance.

"This is more for you than me," she said. "The mountains, the setting when you visit will remind you to pursue the peace and stillness we'll achieve together for you."

"Thanks," I mumbled, not quite sure what to say. I shook my head, eyes tearing. I had been doing a lot of that, both shaking my head and tearing.

"It gets easier," she said, reaching for my hand. "We've lived with the verdict for most of the year, and it has gotten easier to face this."

"But never actually easy."

"Yes," she agreed, "never easy. Disease is not easy. Illness sucks, as the girls would put it. And ALS is just plain awful."

The Mentoring Begins in Earnest

The falling leaves signaled our last holiday season together. Last Thanksgiving. Last Christmas. Last New Year. And still, she smiled. We started the first week of her last six to eight weeks of her internal timetable with a conversation about the need for loving, Spirit-driven action and reaction. The timing was based on her "gut feel" about the progress the "beast in my body" had made.

Her end-of-life arrangements complete, it was time for "heart-to-heart talks about your future." She sat in her wheelchair by the floor-to-ceiling windows in our main room overlooking a wooded ravine and a meandering creek, visible now through the stark winter branches. It was her favorite place to sit, even now in a wheelchair and confined to the house.

"Now it's time to get serious. UVA is saying that I'm going to be able to live into or through the spring, but I don't have that long. I'll probably get through the new year . . . but barely." In touch with her body, guided—as I was increasingly told—by the continuing encouragement and peace of Ps 46, her always-present connection through the stillness of verse 10.

"Pray without ceasing, right?" she asked rhetorically. "So many forms of prayer, and so many places to pray. In a church or synagogue, certainly. Walking along the street. On a treadmill at the fitness center. As long as your mind reaches out into the stillness, that is a form of prayer. Even all day, every day."

She readied me for her passing. At the center of that preparation were the words of God in the tenth verse, the Spirit that flowed into her in the stillness, that personally connected her to the wisdom and hope and optimism of the supernatural—the magic, if you will—universe of his Spirit.

Stillness. So much talk about stillness. So much emphasis on being still.

"You sound like a Quaker," I said. "Sit around together and don't talk."

"Ah, but they *do* talk," she said with a twinkle in her eyes. "Just not to each other."

"Oh—I get it. God stuff."

Over those weeks, she emphasized stillness "because that's where God is best found, that's how he guides and loves. Shut out the phones, the television, the chaos around you, and feel the stillness. I want your life after . . ."

". . . 'I'm gone,'" I interjected, a half-smile on my face. "Got it."

She nodded. "See? You're already being positive. An intimate relationship with the Spirit should produce smiles and ease, regardless of—" She repositioned the wand that suctioned the saliva collecting in her mouth. "—the *stinkin' stuff*."

The Conversation Chair

One evening, early in those first weeks of the last months, I sank exhausted into the upholstered chair by her bed in the room we had equipped for her. She had insisted on that chair, what she called "our conversation chair," which I would use each evening and often through the night to converse by her bedside. And between and after the visits by our girls. But that night, I was exhausted: Work; drive home to assist the health aides; gently lift from bed, place in wheelchair, lift to commode, return to bed; back to work; home again to assist the health aides. Wheelchair, commode, bed. Back to work. Pick up medical supplies. Back to work. Worry. Work. Worry. And finally, at work and in the car, more worry, worry, worry.

The aides had just left. The upholstered wingback chair reassuringly wrapped itself around me as I wearily dropped my feet on the matching ottoman. The early winter sunset barely peeked into the room, leaving it comfortably dim with only two lamps with low-wattage bulbs that were easier on her eyes. I leaned over her and put two drops of artificial tears into each eye, which were dry and irritated from the disease, and adjusted her bed into a more comfortable position for talking.

"I'll bring you out to the big room," I offered. "No food odors at all—I cleaned the kitchen top to bottom last night while you were sleeping."

She had developed an extraordinary sensitivity to food, choking and unable to breathe at even the faintest whiff of food and beverages, or traces of it on someone's breath. I brushed my teeth before coming into the room after work, removing traces of my afternoon coffee, and now routinely had energy bars for my evening meals—paired with a nice pinot noir—out on our screened porch. No more use of the microwave or stove, because when the aroma of food wafted through the house, she choked. Odors, food odors especially, impacted her respiratory system.

"No, I'll stay here," she said, taking in the room with her eyes—much easier than trying to turn her head. "Thanksgiving is coming up, and I want you to get all the rest you can. I tire easily and I can't put my arms around your neck anymore when you lift. Let's just stay here and talk, then I'll sleep."

"My mind keeps running forward, to the New Year. Wish I could turn it off."

"I don't think about it," she said. "I stay in the here and now, working my way through each moment, not thinking about what's ahead."

"Hard to do," I pointed out.

"Yes," Sharon replied, "but doable, especially if you *Ps-46 it.*" She smiled.

"Sort of not sure what you mean," I grumbled wearily, leaning forward in the chair, and then immediately felt guilty. I had let crankiness creep into my voice. I was tired but she was dying; big difference. Wide gap. Guilt, deep sigh (again, and again and again and again), and made ready to project what I actually was and, in fact, had been every day since we'd met: deeply in love.

Time for Positive, Not Weary

I reached over and rested a hand on her hand, which lay cold on the bed. Time for positive, not weary, acutely aware that I needed to be there for her. My guilt, as unreasonable as it was, was ever present as I felt helpless in the face of this disease. Surely, if I were any kind of best friend and lover, any kind of husband I could do something. Anything. Intellectually, I knew how unreasonable those feelings were but, still, they were an ever-present ache. I can't protect you. I can't *do* anything. Guilt and more guilt.

"This is wearing on you, in ways different than me," she whispered.

"Yup," I said, shaking off the guilt and slightly, carefully squeezed her hand.

"*Psalm-46 it,*" she repeated. "Stop. Close your eyes. Be still, sometimes physically but always mentally. The more you internalize this psalm and the discipline of stillness, the less time you'll need to feel the beyond-natural power of a connection to God, and let his Spirit flow into and through you. Be open to the calm it brings, to the spiritual knowledge and savvy available to deal with your immediate situation, directing your feelings and thoughts, and controlling your anxieties."

"*Psalm-46 it* is what you do when you're getting ready to act, to make a decision, to choose a path, when you need the kind of connected calm that concentrates your mind," she rasped. "Or you're seeking simple peace. Stop. Close your eyes. Be still. Stillness is not just a form of prayer; it *is* prayer. Over time, praying becomes ingrained in you and, without thinking, you give The Spirit a chance to guide you. Automatic, as much a part of you as breathing."

"Psalm 46 is a *gateway* psalm, a portal to exploring the mysteries of God's Spirit and the richness of God's word. Those mysteries will impact how you feel, how you look at and react to life. Those mysteries, if you're open to receiving beyond-natural guidance, to lifting your being to another and positive level, will cause you to smile with the realization that everything, every challenge you face is doable. You'll get through it."

She continued. "Feel the bitterness; feel the anger at my, your, our situation melt. God is with us; God is with you long past my . . ." She quietly smiled. "You know the rest."

"Passing?"

"Yes, sweetheart, yes. Psalm-46 your grief, your anger." She took a shuddering breath. "My disease—it is what it is. But your future, that of the girls, all open and filled with opportunity, possibility, and love. God wants us to be positive, to love. Let Ps 46 push you to other parts of his word, use his Spirit to guide you in decisions, in his word, in how and with what emotions you'll remember me. You and the girls, every single person that comes into this room—all of you have so much life left to live. Be positive. Smile. Use Ps 46 as the starting point to live and love your life."

Getting My Head Examined

Later I sought the assistance of a counselor in dealing with the grief of her passing. Real men don't do shrinks? Wrong. Sharon had taught me that real men—and women—are unafraid to love, have faith, and seek help, both from God directly and through his proxies on earth. "Be still and know" that I needed someone to talk with, someone upon whom I could unload my grief, a counselor—Christian or otherwise.

One day, after more than a month of weekly fifty-minute sessions, he leaned forward in his chair and commented, "You may know, I do quite a bit of couples counseling. But listening to you, hearing about Sharon and her approach to marriage and relationships, I have a new outlook. Sharon has affected my other work."

"How so?" I asked, although I was not surprised and already knew the answer. Sharon and her positive, spiritual approach to living had that effect on those open to what some, cynical and spiritually closed, called "naive" or "corny." But it wasn't at all corny and certainly not naive; rather, her way of relationship, a positive approach that—if you were open-minded and listened, really listened, could touch you on a deeper, more spiritual level—was sweet and affecting and, for many around her, life-affirming. Especially her family.

"I have couples who come in and, from the beginning to the end of our session, throw out a litany of complaints. You didn't do this, you didn't do that; I didn't get this, I didn't get that. We never do what I want, just what *you* want. Constant snipping at each other. But now I think about Sharon, about what she went through.

"Faced with a terminal illness, she was more concerned with others and, what appears the ultimate in strength, helping in advance her loved ones deal with her passing and its aftermath. I don't consider myself a religious person. But now I want to say to those couples, find faith. Get some God into your relationships. Be still, take a deep breath, and feel fortunate that you're able to take that breath."

I blinked the tears from my eyes.

"No self-pity, no anger at her lot in life," he continued. "Just acceptance, and love for those around her, and the determination to leave your happiness as her legacy . . .the legacy of faith."

I nodded.

"I've spent so much time when getting my degrees discussing love, reading about love, trying to gain an understanding of it. When you get down to it, my counseling overwhelmingly deals with helping couples learn to accommodate and love each other. And now I think, 'If I could only share the kind of person Sharon was, let them get a glimpse of true love and humility, and grace, all wrapped around faith, her understanding of biblical love . . .'" He trailed off.

And I thought: Quite insightful, despite all those degrees on your wall. That's what I've been telling you, a life significant for not being conventionally significant, a quiet life of quiet love and faith. A bit old-fashioned, even; eschewing controversy and confrontation, pursuing happiness through positive living, through family and God. And yet, contemporary, in the sense that she had overcome so much of the misogyny and stereotyping rampant in this world, from both men and women—and smiled through it all, knowing—absolutely knowing—that God would take care of her. Not the expected answers to prayer all the time, of course, but answers nonetheless and enough spiritual nudges to make a difference. And now, her final challenge: cope with suffering and death in a way that leaves her husband and children positioned for success in what she called "Life After Sharon."

Peace, Inner Joy, and Soul-Rattling Potholes on the Highway of Life

The story of her terminal illness and passing is a tale of a God-connected life, of spirituality and selflessness . . . and the power of taking to heart God's word, all the while relying on a single psalm as a path to discernment and peace in all circumstances.

Spurred on by the truth of God's word, her frequent Bible reading, both Old and New Testaments, and her lifetime embrace of the Forty-Sixth Psalm and the faith and connection emanating from it, she codified what six decades of living—more than half with me—had taught: That yes, there is a way to keep walking, to not get rattled by bumps in the road that range from mild to jarring to bone-crushing and soul-rattling . . . and to smile while drawing upon inner strength and peace. "Remember, God's strength, his Spirit is always there—if you take hold of it."

Although Sharon suffered, she never despaired. Wife and mother first and always, entrepreneur and charities volunteer, she chose to spend her last months on this earth talking through a positive approach to life, her "lessons" that emphasized both outer and inner smiles, a connection to the spiritual love of God through his Word, and her rock-solid faith in his power and purpose. Hers was a very personal faith that allowed her to endure the suffering caused by this debilitating disease with dignity and grace.

Homer Simpson, star of the television's *The Simpsons* and one of our greatest public intellectuals, memorably said, "Donuts. Is there anything they can't do?"

Sharon reminds us that donuts can be applied to faith:

Faith. Psalm 46. Is there anything they can't do?

4

Jew Ain't Kidding!

Thugs and a Chasidic Jew

FROM ORDINARY DECISIONS TO life-threatening situations, the Spirit of God guides in the stillness, the whole of his power outlined in the Forty-Sixth Psalm. The lesson of those last six weeks, of all of Sharon's life. The Spirit talks in the stillness. "Be still and know . . ."

"Even now, here in this bed, I close my eyes and seek guidance. I close my eyes and—whether it be for a second, a minute, a half-hour—let the Spirit of God guide me. It's a process.

"I know—having relied upon Psalm 46 for all of my life, letting it lead where it leads, in God's word and beyond—instinctively what I have to do to best deal with what's in front of me. Close your eyes, block out the chaos of anxiety and jumbled, rushing thoughts. And then, somehow, I don't know how—never push *how* on the Spirit—I open my eyes and feel hope and know, just know, the best path to take . . . which is always something to smile about."

"There are some situations in which you have to react immediately. You can't take the time to look for peace," I pointed out. "Remember the thugs on the playground near grandma's apartment in Brooklyn? They had surrounded your friend, the Chasidic Jew."

She chuckled. "Moshe. Not a friend at first, but he became a friend. Despite my being a woman."

"You stepped into the middle of that! Surely, you had no time to begin 'the process,' as you put it."

Smiles and Muggers

"All it takes is a moment, even a fraction of a second." She smiled. "I closed my eyes, felt the connection through a stillness during which time and events slowed. In the blink of an eye to you—but a slowed, considered pause to me—I knew what had to be done."

"You scared the hell out of me."

"And Grandma Anna, I know. But I couldn't let them hurt Moshe."

"No, you couldn't. That's just not you, never been since I met you and, I'm sure, before."

I had been raised Jewish in New York and Connecticut. That included all the trappings: a kosher household, bar mitzvah, and a quintessentially Jewish mother and grandmother. Grandma Anna had lived in her Brooklyn apartment for decades. But as she aged, it was increasingly difficult for her to get around. Sharon and I would periodically stop by her apartment and drive her up to visit my parents in Connecticut. The highlight of our visits would be Grandma Anna insisting on "a nosh before we go." This invariably included gefilte fish and chopped chicken livers, topped off by Entenmann's cakes and a walk to the nearby park to let her friends know that her grandchildren "are wonderful" and taking her to visit her daughter in Connecticut.

We'd sit on a bench as she visited with friends, while men in kippahs held in place by bobby pins played handball on the courts behind us. Over time, Sharon had befriended an elderly Chasidic Jew, intrigued by his davening Jewish prayers. She was especially fascinated by the mysticism inherent in his constant movement. He would periodically rise up to stand in front of the bench, swaying back and forth while praying in a barely discernable chant. Weather permitting, he was always at the park when we visited, and over two years became quite talkative—to Sharon—about the mystery of davening the Bible as prayer. Sharon had that *way* about her, smiling and encouraging others to talk, even a set-in-his-ways patriarchal Orthodox Jew who kept his distance from women. Score: Smiles 1, Patriarchy 0.

But by the mid-eighties the neighborhood was rapidly changing, with many of the Jewish shops closing their doors. Graffiti, booze, and drugs, not handball and chess played on concrete tables with embedded game surfaces, were the order of the day in the tiny park. Fewer kippahs, more profanity drove elderly Jews to hide behind the heavy doors of their apartments, a brave few venturing into the park only during the height of the day and not for long. The handball courts had been taken over by skateboarders and dope dealers, and profane screams had largely replaced the quiet, rhythmic chants of old men davening, and the slap-clop of handball.

Into this we walked one day, passing the corner of her apartment building which bordered the park, as Grandma Anna wanted to tell "my friend Esther I'll be gone to Connecticut for a week." We would drive her up, and my dad, her son-in-law, would take her back. "She lives across the hall. We watch out for each other."

The park came into sight. The tiny, baggy black-suited figure of Moshe framed by four youths, all gang tattoos and muscles, one holding his arm while another waved a gleaming straight-edge razor. Another menacingly waved a skateboard over his head.

We stopped short at the entrance to the park.

"You take Grandma Anna back to the apartment and call the police," I whispered urgently. "I'll wait here for them."

No reply. I looked over at Sharon. Her eyes were closed. Seconds passed and they blinked open. Out of the stillness. She smiled, shaking her head.

"No, *you* take Grandma Anna back. Call the police. Moshe is my friend." Her smile grew wider and, before I could utter a word of protest, she walked quickly but casually into the playground. I heard her call out to Moshe, a genuine smile of pleasure on her face, not a trace of anxiety. She stepped calmly up to her friend, took his arm, and turned to the youths—thugs, really.

They were chanting: "Jew! Jew! Jew!"

Sharon waited. The chants faded. The thug with a razor turned to her.

"Hey, lady, you want some of this." You could see a light bulb turn on in his head—an extremely dim one. He turned to the others, who were still holding Moshe, and nastily said, "Hey lady, *Jew* want some of this?" They laughed uproariously—good joke!

Sharon looked at them, smiling easily, ignoring the razor, the skateboards and spray paint. "Everybody likes Moshe, I know." she smiled easily.

She stepped forward, brushing aside the youth with a razor. Then she gently lifted their hands from his arms. They froze. "I know you want him to stay here. But he promised to have lunch with us and chopped liver doesn't keep."

Skateboard stepped forward, a menacing look on his face. "Hey . . ."

"Later," she interrupted, "later."

With that, she softly tugged on Moshe's arm and walked him deliberately, as quickly as a ninety-year-old can walk, from their midst and across the park. She smiled all the while. The youths stared, mouths open and frozen in place by surprise. I half expected her to stop to admire the flowers . . . except this was a Brooklyn Park maintained—to be generous—by the city, which had cultivated a fine crop of broken glass and syringes.

She brought Moshe over to us, and we walked slowly away. When the four of us turned the corner of Grandma Anna's apartment building and were out of sight, I quietly asked, "'Chopped liver doesn't keep'? Really? That's the best you could do?"

The smile that had extricated the frail old man widened. "Hey, it was the first thing that came to mind."

When You're Connected, It Only Takes a Moment

Sharon, from her bed, recalled the incident. "When we saw what was happening, I closed my eyes. *Shalom*, peace becomes instinctive, preparing the ground for the next steps. I needed only a moment." She looked at me. "Get good at this, get used to calling upon your personal spiritual connection, and that moment will expand or contract to fit the decisions and actions you need. 'Be still and know that I am God!' Other verses from Ps 46 flowed, in a jumbled order—just what I needed when I needed. I knew immediately that the only thing to do was walk in, be as non-threatening as possible, and then walk out with Moshe.

"He was so rattled, so surprised by how quickly everything was happening, he let me hold his arm and walk him away. A woman, and not his wife! Somehow the energy of my connection to the Spirit overcame his legalistic interpretation of God's word, that men may touch only their wives . . . even in this situation. Somehow, once I had closed my eyes, I knew that that was the way to go, both with Moshe and those boys."

"They weren't boys. They were vicious thugs."

"Yes, but I just had a feeling they weren't all complete sociopaths. Something told me they were cowards deep down, and I could take advantage of that if I acted quickly. Besides, maybe only one was a sociopath, and surprise was a factor."

"Surprise was certainly a factor for the rest of us. You really scared Grandma Anna . . . and me."

"I'm scared now when I think about it. But then, in that instant of hesitation, a calm flowed through me, and I had a picture of what I had to do. I knew that God was my refuge and strength."

"More Ps 46," I nodded. "How about 'always ready to help in times of trouble'?"

"You've been doing your homework. Except that should be updated, 'always ready to help when faced with antisemitic thugs.' I knew it would work out, and that it wouldn't be too long before we were sharing a glass of schnapps, Moshe's favorite drink. Remember, that's the first thing Moshe asked for when we got him up to Grandma Anna's apartment?"

"Never did have our chopped chicken livers," I remembered.

Sharon put on a mock-serious face. She loathed liver dishes, in any form from any animal. "Thank God."

And then she smiled, a smile as wide as her dying muscles would allow.

The Spirit, Anti-Semitism, and Calm

Then we took up where we had left off with Sharon explaining why she had been able to defuse the situation with Moshe and the anti-Semitic thugs.

"What struck me that day was your calm," I complimented. "You simply did what you thought you needed to do despite knowing you and Moshe could get seriously hurt, perhaps even murdered." That was not hyperbole; this was New York City, where muggings and murders were and now, even more so, a fact of life. "That pause at the park entrance?! That's what you're talking about, isn't it, when you closed your eyes? *Psalm-46 it*, right? 'The Spirit worked in me, during that slight pause before I opened my eyes.'"

She chuckled hoarsely, "In that moment, not only did I know what to do, but I knew, knew with certainty, that I had little to fear."

She closed her eyes and picked from her memory this verse in Ps 46: "'So we will not fear when earthquakes come and the mountains crumble into the sea.'"

She continued: "I opened my mind and reached out in the stillness, opening my heart and soul to the Spirit, knowing that the 'river' of the Spirit 'brings joy to the city of our God.' The city is my mind, my soul. My personal connection brought certain knowledge that he *is* God, that I could smile in the face of the anti-Semitic evil in that park. The Spirit is in me, the beyond-natural voice and strength of God speaks to me in the stillness and connection, and I will not be hurt. God dwells in *me*; *I* cannot be destroyed. From the very break of day, God will protect *me*.' In that stillness, that's where I received direction, boldness, and instruction. Me— the natural—connecting to God through his Spirit, receiving the strength and discernment of the supernatural."

"But you could have been hurt," I pointed out. "Those were dangerous men, perhaps sociopaths."

"Physically, yes. But my heart, my soul urged me on. It may not have been the smartest thing I've ever done, but it was over quickly and all ended well."

"But if it had not?"

"But it did, this time. I've had times when a situation didn't end well, but still, the Spirit brings what I need to make the choices that will best help me through; sometimes perseverance, other times boldness, and growing discernment."

"So let me understand this," I said. "God knows the way forward. All I need to do is be still, take a moment out of my dread now for your suffering, for the grief I'll experience after you're gone, and force my mind . . ."

"Not so much your mind as your heart. And not force. Let go. Listen with an open heart, sweetheart. Heart, soul, spirit, all the same: so many ways to describe the same thing; a voice, an urge in the silence. What some have called the 'light within, the *Shekinah* of the soul.' In the stillness a light comes on and illuminates a path."

I nodded, shifting in the chair. Lot of time in that chair. "So, what you're saying: his Spirit arrives in the stillness with guidance when you have decisions to make, when you need a path; with courage when you need courage; with boldness when you need boldness; peace when you need tranquility; and love when you need to feel loved. But underlying all is a discernment and stability that goes beyond what we have naturally available to us."

Pushing Back the Dark

I looked out the window. The front yard had grown dark, the streetlights now throwing dim shadows off the trees to the side of the lawn. We were on the edge of night, a time when all of our pains, worries and fears are magnified.

Yet, she smiled. And her smile pushed back the dark and uncertainty.

"You're so calm now, facing this disease," I said. "You were so calm that day, while I was scared, Grandma Anna terrified. But you, cool and calm, waded in. For more than thirty years, as long

43

as I've known you, you've had an unnatural calm. How were you so calm? How can you be so calm?"

"How can I be so calm? Just about every visitor asks it; and if they don't ask it, they want to ask it." Again, the smile. "I'm calm because, long ago, I made Ps 46 my own. Psalm 46, then other portions of his word. I took it to heart, all of its elements, and used it to establish a personal relationship with him through his Spirit. I have *shalom*."

Achieving *Shalom*

Shalom, the Hebrew word that describes a deeper, lasting content-ment, derives from an ancient mystical state of inner peace period-ically reached by observant Hebrews—Jews—over the centuries. It characterized the worshipful grace of the Sons of Korah, who cre-ated the psalm as they sat in the temple in Jerusalem, looking back on the tortuous wanderings and trials of the now-freed Egyptian slaves, Hebrews, in the desert so long ago; at the struggles and sins of God's new nation, at the three-steps-forward-two-steps-back (with the occasional three-steps-forward-four-steps back thrown in) dance of humanity. The book of Exodus, more Bible stuff.

"It's more than peace. Psalm 46, memorized and applied correctly, gives you *shalom*, a peace wrapped in contentment, in-ner joy, and the Spirit-driven courage to face whatever the world throws at you. The Jews have always had a deep streak of mysti-cism," she pointed out, "a major advantage of memorizing Ps 46 and applying it, a personalized process of the supernatural applied to the natural."

"You're smiling," I observed.

"The beast in me be damned," she gasped. "*Psalm-46 it* . . . flint hitting steel, producing sparks that lead to fire. That's God, that's faith."

"Whoa! You've become quite poetical in your old age," I joked.

"Have to be. Have to get in everything I can now, as my old age will end soon. Trying every which way to have an impact on you, and quickly."

A Legacy of Smiles and Concern for Others

Sharon, her *shalom* on display in that bed, amazed her healthcare aides with her sunny disposition and focus on them, getting to know them and patiently listening as they talked about themselves. After her passing, one young aide, perhaps, put it best, posting unbidden to Sharon's memorial site hosted by the funeral home.

The aide, Crystal, a single mother raising three children on a limited budget, spent many hours by Sharon's side, enjoying her company and the positive energy that—even while unable to sit, to do all that we take for granted without assistance—still marked Sharon's relationship with others.

Crystal later shared the experience of tending to her dying patient in a funeral home website:

> I met Mrs. Schwartz shortly before her death and was only able to get to know her for about two weeks. But in that short period of time, I learned so how to live my life. She was understanding, soft spoken, and a gentle soul, but most of all so very strong. I came to care very deeply for her. Other then [*sic*] her beautiful smile the one memory that stands out was the day when I told her I had thought about her the night before and explained to her I wouldn't know what to do if I were in her shoes. She looked at me with tears in her eyes and said "If I didn't have Jesus Christ in my heart, I'd be scared to death, but he is here and I am not scared, I am okay." I cried for her, I cried at how strong she is, and I cry every time I think about that day. She is in a better beautiful place, where there is no more pain, no more suffering, and where she can get plenty of rest. I wish I had more time with her but the short time I got to know her was such a blessing. My condolences go out to her husband and two beautiful daughters she shared so many memories about with me,

and my condolences to all family and friends. She will
truly be missed.

The secret of her tranquility? Knowing that God "has my
back."

He has your back, too, she instructed. "Memorize Ps 46.
'Be still and know . . .' when facing the *stinkin' stuff* of life, especially your grief, and then, with your personal connection to the
Spirit arising from that knowledge, let Ps 46 talk *to*—and God
with—you."

5

Hell, I Tell You

Hell, I Tell You

"I've known that you had an affinity for that psalm," I said. "But I didn't know how much a part of your life it's been. So, to you, Ps 46 has had power beyond words on a page in the Bible?"

"Power, yes," she said. "But only in the sense that you access extraordinary and wise guidance from God's world, the beyond-natural world. My reverence for Ps 46 has had everything to do with the awesome power of God, who helps us both persevere and overcome, which I discovered as a little girl."

She turned slightly to me, bunching up the washcloth she used to catch saliva when neither of us could get the suction wand to her mouth quickly enough. She got a far-away look in her eye as she recalled her discovery of the power of the psalm. "I was seven years old, maybe eight; I don't know my exact age then, it's a bit of a blur—and my mom, single, had to work every day to support us, certainly during the week but often on Saturdays."

"We've talked about it. Your dad died when you were two years old, and your mom raised you by herself. She held a series of minimum wage and less jobs. Between what she earned and what the sitters cost, you were barely getting by." I tapped her arm. "See, I've listened!"

She smiled. "Okay, now I'd like you to listen again, so that you understand what Ps 46 and verse 10 in particular has meant for my life, and what it could mean for your life.

"Until I was five, my mother was paying sitters to stay with me at our home. But that had become too expensive, and mom arranged to have me stay at what you would loosely, very loosely, describe as childcare in one of the towns within driving distance of where she worked. I cycled through a bunch of those arrangements.

"The reason I say very loosely is that when we think of a child-care center, we think of nice clean buildings, lots of toys, children playing under supervision, maybe even learning to read and doing other educational exercises that will them help in school. But in so many small towns in West Virginia, childcare was and is someone's home where people pick up extra money for watching children for the day. Not childcare, but being left in someone's care. There's a difference. Sometimes they're good for the kids; much of the time, perhaps most of the time, they're not. I suppose they're better now, what with the different regulations and all, but things were a lot looser then, especially in rural areas, and one of the homes—there were so many—I stayed at was terrible. A self-proclaimed minister and his nasty wife. I went there full-time for a couple of years, and then later was dropped off each day when I got out of school until finally, when I was nine years old, Mom thought I was old enough to stay at our house by myself." She chuckled; a chuckle made grim not just by the pained hoarseness of her voice but by the memories of the succession of people with whom she had been left while her mom worked.

She recounted one couple. "My care was terrible. It was run by an unhappy and vicious couple, 'The Rev' and his wife, who enjoyed punishing us."

"'The Rev'?"

"Short for 'reverend,' I'm sure. Lot of screaming about hell and damnation, his view of the Bible. I don't know that he was an actual minister or just said he was one. Even today, a lot of men claim the status of clergy. Read the Bible once and you're an expert; twice and you're a minister. Or don't read the Bible, but spout off a few phrases." She closed her eyes. "'The Rev' put me off Christians for a long time. Child abuse accompanied by Bible verses. The Bible may be the most-read book in the world, but it's also the most misused."

"True," I sighed. "God, especially, is vulnerable to being turned into a weapon."

"Phonies, all of them that claim power in his name."

The Power of Closing Your Eyes

I shook my head.

"Well, it was cheap and all mom could afford. I remember the chain-link fence, the bare earth dotted with weeds, and some greasy pots and pans for playing. Some real toys, almost all damaged and many rusted, others with the plastic made faded and brittle by the sun. 'The Rev' screamed at us. So did his wife. Dirty, scraggly hair, stained sleeveless shirt that she wore week in and week out, putting a greasy sweatshirt over it in the cold before winter.

"She sat on the front porch all day through most of three seasons, squeezing her enormous body into a webbed aluminum chair, watching her television which was propped on a wooden crate, an extension cord run into the house through a window. She sometimes watched us, which we hated, because she'd scream at us, leaving the hitting to 'The Rev' as she called him, but mostly eating and drinking. I never wanted to remember, or expose you and the girls to the ugliness. You simply didn't need to know. But I'm talking about it now because we're running out of time, because I want to impress upon you the power of Ps 46, which I used to get through it. Psalm 46, memorize it, apply it, and have a great life after . . ."

". . . 'I'm gone,'" I interjected with a sad smile.

"I lived in a different world. You grew up in New York City and the suburbs of Connecticut. A mom and dad, in Jewish communities that emphasized education and 'rightness.' There were exceptions, sure, but that was the rule. Very different from my childhood. Our girls have had every advantage we could afford to give them. Great schools, nice suburbs, beautiful homes. I mean, you and I sent the girls to Montessori and then public schools, when public schools had high standards. Our childcare, Montessori, was amazing, better than any public or private school at any level in my part of West Virginia.

"That was so far from a tiny fenced yard, loaded with screaming kids, a piece of white bread with peanut butter for snacks, for lunch, every day. No plates or napkins; hold out your hands and take your single piece of bread with just a whisper of peanut butter. And don't complain, to them or to your parents, or you may end up with no snacks, no lunch, and maybe thrown out. In which case, my mom would lose pay while she figured out where to park me next."

"I'm sorry you had to go through all that," I said one night.

"Yes, 'The Rev' used Bible verses as weapons that accompanied his swings at us after pointing out transgressions, imaginary or otherwise. 'You have dirt on your knees . . . "Wash yourself and be clean,'" he'd quote—*whack!* 'You spilled your water . . . "You careless ones will care, for your fruit crops will fail,"' shouting a Bible passage in what I'd learned later was proof-texting—*swat!!!* 'I told you to hold it, you don't have to pee . . . "Those who respect a command will succeed"'—*slap!!!*"

She continued. "But then I had a life-changing discovery. I was playing with another girl, obviously enjoying ourselves. Our squeals of delight grew louder and louder, attracting his attention. That was a no-no; you didn't want to attract the attention of either him or his wife. He put down his can of beer, came down off the porch, and grabbed my arm. He cocked his fist, then hit me on the side of the head, knocking me to the ground, at the same time screaming 'Be still and know that I am God!' Standing over me, he repeated it: 'Be STILL and know that I am God!' He angrily stomped away. I lay on the ground, silently crying, trying to clear my head of the bright spots and dark that had exploded behind my eyes after he hit me. Looking back, maybe I had a concussion."

I stared at her, feeling the horror of an adult striking a small child, of the "care" she had experienced.

She continued: "At first, I couldn't see anything except those spots. But behind those spots, 'Be still and know that I am God' echoed in my mind. When my sight returned, and I was on my back, looking up at the gray sky. Sunshine was rare in the mountains that time of year, and most days were overcast. But then, something within me, at once both alien and comfortable, within my seven-year-old self said, 'Close your eyes again, don't look.'

"I closed my eyes, and then the wonder happened. A little girl, flat on the ground, face up, eyes closed to the low-hanging clouds, and I was free to create any kind of world I wanted. 'Be still and know that I am God!' he had said. That's what he shouted when he hit me. But my mind—my soul, I now know—latched on to those words, reciting them over and over as I lay there. They brought a peace that I had never known, and the certainty that I would get through this. A Bible verse that he had used to hit me with his fist, that I'd heard him shout a hundred times before when kids got lively; but this time, on the bare earth with my eyes closed, something happened. Something good. Then, eyes closed and face to the sky, still on the ground, I smiled. I knew that he and his wife wouldn't defeat me, couldn't defeat me, that someone was helping me out, and that whatever terrible things happened in that childcare, I would work through."

"But when you opened your eyes, reality was still there," I pointed out.

"True, but *I* was different. *My* reality had changed. My circumstances were unchanged, but my perception of those circumstances had changed. An internal peace, helped along by a blow to the head, had blocked out the abuse and chaos and reality I faced as a little girl in that yard. I had hope.

"I never knew," I repeated, shaking my head. "We never talked about it."

"Our marriage, our life together with the girls has been happy. You've been a wonderful husband—except when you weren't . . ."

"Hey," I interrupted. "Are you saying I'm not perfect?"

"What do you think?" she teased.

"How does that relate to Ps 46 beyond the verse he used to hit children having too much fun?"

"That night at home I asked Mom while she was fixing our dinners if she had ever heard the phrase 'Be still and know that I am God.' She nodded, told me that it was somewhere in the book of Psalms, didn't know exactly where, and then turned back to the stove. I went into the other room, opened Mom's Bible, and looked up the verse. It took me a more than a week to find it—I was a good reader, ahead of my age, but still a child. I went psalm by psalm, sounding every verse out, until I found Ps 46."

"I bet it was the King James version," I said. "That's tough reading even if you're an adult. All that 'thee, thou, thy' stuff."

"No, not that I remember. It was hard to read, but mainly because I wasn't used to it. But something kept me going until I found Ps 46. I read it over and over, and discovered the context of the tenth verse. Not an easy thing to do for a seven-year-old girl. I kept at it, continuing the night I discovered the psalm and the passage that floated in my head while I was on the ground. I read and reread that psalm each evening while mom was making dinner, and each time felt something stir in me, reassure me. The blow to the head had knocked me silly; but now I understood the feeling of strength and comfort that had washed over me as I lay on the ground, catching my breath, eyes closed to block out the ugliness.

"Yes, I had the occasional bruise from getting whacked, a big one that day; and yes, I had headaches. But now I had hope and the knowledge that things would change, perhaps every day, that my time in that yard would not last forever. It was the only thing I read for the next month, and I became stronger than ever. I was convinced, as I struggled through Ps 46 each evening . . ."

"No television?"

"Didn't get television until I was about nine years old. Rabbit ears, West Virginia mountains, a television left out in a neighbor's trash, and a single station that drifted in and out of focus. Television? Not then. Just a Bible and determination. Within a few days I understood that the verse he yelled when he punched me—week-in and week-out, he liked to hit us—was a gateway to strength and perseverance. With God's help, we can both endure and thrive. God instilled in a skinny child, all stick legs and arms, strength out of the stillness, in the bruise on the side of her head. His Spirit connected to me, each time I read that psalm at the end of the day, it gave a little girl hope and the certainty that she was no longer powerless."

"Makes sense," I said. "It slowed you down, giving you room to breathe. And a connection to someone more powerful than the circumstances you faced."

"That held me in good stead throughout the years, through so many of the crises of my life. And then of our life together. Close your eyes when the waters are flooding over you. The Spirit is always there, connecting. At childcare, I was a child and powerless, so I endured it, often shutting my eyes and being still, knowing that there would be a better life for me someday. I was protected."

"How does that help now?"

Anticipating Grief

Her eyes, alive and glistening, turned to me. "For you, simple. I will have died. You will have nursed me through this, with no hope of a cure. The ALS will have run its course. A funeral. Anger, sorrow, tears. Grief, intense grief. But, when everyone has gone, close your eyes and concentrate, summon up other images, other ways to move forward. By then you'll have memorized Ps 46, and at least have a start toward the spiritual bond that comes from knowing God. Embrace the quiet. Gain strength. In the dark, behind your eyes, knowing which way to go next, the path, will come to you. You'll have help, always help, regardless of the reality you face when, as you will inevitably do, you open your eyes."

"Deny reality?

"No, enhance it. Augment it. Shut your eyes and imagine. God gave us both self-awareness and the ability to choose between paths. When you open your eyes, the world will still be there, but now your perceptions will have changed. In the dark behind your eyes comes the realization that now is not forever, that now is always changes, and you're capable of directing and guiding those changes. And when you can't direct and guide, you can endure. Use that calm, that peace, to look for the opening inside you, that place where you can find the door to another world, his world, the one where all of life originates and is driven by spiritual energy. A Spirit that is there to help. Breathe deeply; feel the Spirit, taste the Spirit, talk with the Spirit."

"I understand . . . but I'm not sure I'm strong enough to do it after all"—I swung my arm around, taking in the room of medical devices—"this."

"Force yourself to smile at least once after I'm gone. Then again. And again. Read Ps 46, as I did—again and again, committing it to memory—and I promise you, it will get easier, and the world will get brighter. I promise."

"Tough to do," I replied.

She drew a deep breath. "You have no idea."

"Secrets?"

"Not really," she said. "Just things that were better left unsaid, that hurt too much to talk about. And had no relevance whatsoever to our happy, very happy life together. We've had our ups and down, as any good marriage will have. But our commitment, faith, and respect for each other and God led to an underlying happiness. But now, it's time to talk about what brought me to this point, that I can still smile, if only to reinforce the power of Ps 46."

I looked at her quizzically.

She turned her eyes away. "My discovery of 'be still' and Ps 46 gave me the strength to endure sexual abuse in a shed in that same yard, to later overcome some poor choices as a young adult, and yet, later, have a life of love with you and the girls. All of you, our memories that we made together, replaced those poisoned memories."

Evil and Good

I was stunned into silence. Sexual abuse?!

She continued, slowly and matter-of-factly. "I've had a life-time of living with this, for most of my years tucked deep in the recesses of my mind. It's ugly, ugly, ugly . . . but I've never been haunted by it. My discovery of the spiritual and healing powers of Ps 46—and later, the Bible—allowed me to overcome something that could have, would have haunted me all of my life. But even as a child I was determined to not let it ruin my future."

The air in the room suddenly became stifling. "You never said a word in all these years."

"There was no reason to. You, me, and the girls lived a sane and ordinary life, a fulfilling life, a good life . . ."

"Not without its challenges," I noted.

She momentarily closed her eyes, gathering strength. "True," she repeated. "Not without its challenges. But we faced normal challenges that any normal family faces. I just loved our lifestyle, loved our girls, loved all the different vacations we were able to go on. And I loved loving. I've heard so many times that God is love; that's tough to wrap your mind around because it's a generalization. Generic love. It's when it gets down to the specifics of who you love, what you love, how you treat others—that's when you see, taste, and feel love, God's love."

"So how does Ps 46 enter into this?"

"Psalm 46: I have his assurance that, ultimately, he is on my side. I can smile because 'God is our refuge and strength,' he is 'always ready to help in times of trouble.' I can deal with the injustices of life because I 'will not fear when earthquakes come and the mountains crumble into the sea.' I look on that moment of stillness that's in verse 10 as a way to specifically and spiritually connect to the love of God: 'A river brings joy to the city of our God, the sacred home of the Most High.' That city is my body, even when it was violated . . ."

I swallowed, my eyes tearing. "But . . ."

She raised her hand as much as the disease would allow. "Let me finish. Your joy, getting over the grief of my passing, depends upon this, establishing that spiritual connection in the stillness and allowing God's 'River of Joy' to course through your existence, washing away the grief, knowing that his Spirit 'dwells in that city'—you—and 'cannot be destroyed. From the very break of day,' God will protect you. During this time of my life, I knew—knew! —that he was there, protecting me."

"But . . ."

She interrupted. "Put it this way: I wasn't scarred by the ugliness of abuse to the point where I couldn't function as your wife and the mother of our girls. Because . . . Ps 46."

"And you're telling me this now—why?" The room was quiet, the only sound the hum of the medical devices.

Memorize Psalm 46 and Use It!

"Because I want you to understand the power that Ps 46 had, and has in keeping me going, of allowing me to get through and beyond this evil and others . . ."

"Others? More that I don't know." I shook my head.

"Later," she said pointedly. "Now, I'm asking you to memorize the psalm. God did not allow what I went through over the years to ruin my life, and neither will your life be ruined by my passing. Memorize Ps 46, apply the process by beginning with verse 10, and draw strength and wisdom from whatever then the Spirit puts in your mind. Memorize and then *Ps-46 it*, and your grief will be put in perspective. You'll feel *shalom*, peace."

Despite the seriousness of our conversation, I chuckled. "*Shalom*. My Jewishness has rubbed off on you."

Be Still: Close Your Eyes and Let *Shalom* Flow

She took a shallow breath. "*Shalom* is Hebrew for peace and much more. And it is intimately connected to Ps 46. *Shalom* refers to well-being, to good health. When you wish someone '*Shalom*' you are praying for them to enjoy the internal peace, happiness, and security that comes through the grace of God, through faith that obstacles will be overcome and that—whether now or later—all will be well. Prayer can be a single word or many; that's the key to be always praying, always staying connected to God and his Spirit. Breathe that positive spiritual energy through you, completely filling your body. *Shalom* is an important layer in the strength and discernment the psalm gives you."

"What you went through makes me sick. Sexual abuse?" I brought my hand to my forehead. "I want you to tell me about it, but I don't."

"Yes, I understand. I feel the same way. Sick to my stomach, fear, anxiety, rage, helplessness—all of that together, each in turn. But, in a strange way, I was fortunate that he liked quoting Bible verses when he hit us. Because that led the way to Ps 46, and the rest of God's word. His doing that had nothing to do with God, but everything to do with the cruel games that he liked to play. But evil stuff, *stinkin' stuff* happens. Much of what we endure is evil; that's what I've faced, then as a little girl and later as a young woman. But his use of 'Be still and know that I am God' sent me to my mom's Bible, touching off a lifetime of security and feelings of being loved, whatever the situation. My stomach turns when I think of it. But it all turned out to the good."

She moved one knee slightly; all she could manage. "Even when your body stops responding, when you're living with the physical and emotional pain, you can be still be reassured." She tapped the Bible at her side. "God with us. Psalm 46, a way of life. The tenth verse, our ticket to the happily-ever-after."

She smiled; weakly, but an encouraging and reassuring smile.

6

More Hell, More Abuse

Hell and Motor Oil

SHARON WAS TIRING, BUT that didn't stop her from continuing. We were about a third of the way through what she, with wry humor called *The Last Days of Sharon* ("Makes for a great book title, doesn't it? Or movie," she added, a touch of laughter in her voice). She closed her eyes, resting and gathering strength.

After about two minutes, she continued, "And now, as Paul Harvey used to say, 'the rest of the story.'"

"We can wait until you've slept," I said.

"Not yet," she said. "Just move the chair closer. I want to finish."

She closed her eyes, resting while I moved the heavy, upholstered chair.

"He had a shed in the back, a ramshackle affair, where he kept a rusty old lawnmower and a disorganized, dirty mess of tools that he used to work on his car." She worked her head to the side. "Filth, disorder. Evil always likes filth and disorder. There was also a small couch with mold on it, smelling of grass clippings, grease, and oil. It was a private place where he retreated from the bedlam of the children and the nagging of his wife, a vicious shrew. Occasionally referred to her as 'the devil's whore.' Thought he was clever. Sterling guy, right? Trash, just trash! All of them. For me, hell and motor oil."

I said nothing. I had a feeling of foreboding in the pit of my stomach.

You Can't Feng Shui Depravity

"Friends would come by from time to time. Those who dropped by the shed, at least when I was there, were always male, always unwashed hair and wearing greasy caps, stained by decades of sweat; soiled T-shirts and wife-beaters that had never seen the inside of a washing machine; the outside matched the inside, where personal hygiene went to die."

"Getting eloquent in your old age," I gently joked, just to relieve the building tension.

"Have to use it, my sense of humor," she replied. "Remember, I'm on a deadline."

"I love you."

"And I love you," she said, and continued. "Our love: Heaven. Dealing with them: Hell. I remember body odor and bad teeth. Yellow teeth. Brown teeth stained by tobacco. Missing teeth. Sometimes they'd sit on the front porch, drinking beer, laughing, and yelling. The kids would go to the other side of the yard when they visited. Same rules as a prison with sadistic guards, I'd imagine—don't let them notice you. Don't stand out.

"Most times, however, they'd go into the shed, away from The Rev's wife and her television. Once in a while, when he could barely walk, the 'The Rev' staggered out into the yard and grabbed one of us, the kids, by the arm and dragged them to the shed. I've been told I was a beautiful child—I don't know, and I don't really care about such things. But I tended to be grabbed more often than the others. Once in the shed, he'd tighten his hold on my arm, and throw me on the plywood floor across from them; the floor was gross, covered in grease and oil. Then they'd continue drinking, all the while making rude, sleazy comments. I won't repeat the comments—I don't want them floating in this room."

"I understand," I said.

"I love our home, my room," she said. "Much better than hospice. This is where I want to be right now, and I don't want this floating in the air; you can't *feng shui* depravity."

"No, you can't. Better not to go into it."

"Probably," she agreed. "But I want you to understand where I'm coming from when I ask you to memorize and use Ps 46, that the result will lead you into a fulfilled and thriving life after . . ."

". . . 'I'm gone,'" I finished. "Trying to understand."

"You will—just be patient." She smiled sadly and said, in a low voice, "Be still and listen. You'll understand. Depravity, yes; a sea of depravity. But you'll understand how faith, how God's word became a life saver. One friend in particular, a nasty and cruel man—I'd say animal but animals are extraordinarily civilized by comparison. They are who they are, natural. But these men: Cruelty and evil, as only humans can be."

"I know." The beginnings of nausea, a sinking feeling in anticipation of what I would hear.

"He liked to expose himself to me while the others cheered him on. Disgusting people doing and saying disgusting things." The revulsion on her face was palpable, even in the gloom. "The first time he was too drunk to do anything more than look at me and make rude slurs. But the next time, he grabbed me off the floor and pushed me down on his lap. He opened his zipper and exposed himself. And did other things. Again, the sexual slurs, all the while fondling himself. And me. Beer and motor oil.

"It escalated. My memories are all beer and motor oil and being touched in places a child should not be touched in. At times, he pulled my hand over and made me touch him. Sometimes I'd have to touch others. It wasn't long before they were doing . . ." she paused.

Silence hung over the room like thunderclouds over the Blue Ridge mountains.

"It wasn't long before they were doing other things," she whispered, her voice breaking as the memories worked their way to the surface. "I cried at first, it hurt so much. But, as the months passed, I didn't give in to the pain . . . the utter depravity, the horror. After that first week, I refused to cry. Whimper? Yes, like a wounded animal. But cry? No. That would be giving in, and so I turned up the volume inside my head on Ps 46, and allowed the certainty of a better future push back the pain, the knowledge that—at some point—this would end."

I said nothing. I thought nothing. But my stomach churned.

"Those trips to the shed would come back to haunt us later, in our marriage, when intimacy was so difficult for me."

"But . . ."

She slowly raised her hand, all bones and flesh, and laid it on the bedrail.

I was stunned. I hung head my head and stared at the floor, filled with anger and disgust and shame that people do that—and more—to children. I knew then and know now that it happens: Cognitive knowledge, right, distanced from emotion?

But listening to my bedridden best friend, my partner and lover of more than three decades brought depravity and evil home. There in the darkened room, an eerie glow cast by a small artificial Christmas tree offered by a visitor hoping to bring cheer, and monitors on the many medical devices, her horrific tale unwound. I couldn't move; it was as if the room was filled with the souls of all the children down through the millennia who had suffered this and other forms of barbarism and cruelty: infants and toddlers slaughtered in the Nazi concentration camps; children raped and savaged in the Rwandan genocide of the nineties; the criminals shooting and knifing their way through the children of our cities; and so much more. And so, I sat, for the moment, helpless and hopeless.

She sensed my feelings. "I'm telling you this because I want you to understand that, even in the worst of circumstances, there is hope. Live in faith. Keep the faith, sweetheart—as you say, 'trite but true.'"

No Room for Despair

"Don't despair," she said. "No need to say anything. I had Ps 46 in my mind, always playing in the background, always when Mom dropped me off, in the yard, and always in that shed. So much happened to me in that shed before I could convince my mom that it was time to let me stay at our home alone. Of course, I didn't tell her the reason. I just insisted, I'm a big girl and could look after myself."

"Why didn't you tell her?"

"I didn't want her to be burdened by that knowledge; she had enough on her plate, barely able to take care of a daughter. She worked all the time. She was lonely and bitter since my dad died and, no matter how much she tried to hide it, her unhappiness showed. You can't hide those things—kids know. I was the one bright spot in her life. She needed a bright spot, and I didn't want to have her looking at me in any way knowing that I had been involved in that . . . that . . . that garbage. Anyway, she would have called the police and, in the end, it would be my word against theirs. I didn't want to go through that, as a little girl. I would be forever tainted, in her eyes and the eyes of others. And given that we lived in a small town, everyone would know—and, no matter what anyone would say to the contrary, she'd be forever shamed. And I was dealing with feelings of guilt. No matter who you are, no matter your age, you have shame tinged by guilt. Makes no sense, right? What did I do?"

"Seven years old. You had these evil things happening to you for more than a year?" I nodded. "I understand. How would you know who to turn to, if not your mom?"

"I didn't know what to do and I surely did not want to burden her," she said quietly, the dusk of winter closing in around us. "She looked out for me, but I looked out for her. Should I have insisted? Maybe. I didn't know then, and thinking back I still I don't know. I kept at her though, telling her I wanted to stay at our house. No more childcare, adults supposedly looking out for kids. Just didn't want to go back to that house. And I prayed Ps 46. Day after day.

Week after week. Month after month. Finally, she allowed me to stay home after school, saving her the cost of paying for my care—if that's what you want to call it."

No More Babies

"Your mom . . ."

"Didn't know. Didn't tell her. Never, ever. It would have killed her. And I would never have told you, except that I think it's now a way to sear Ps 46 into your mind, and impress upon you how serious I am about this approach. Before today, I did not want to talk about this . . . this . . . this stuff. I didn't want those violations to be any part of our life together, nor did I see any reason to allow that to enter your mind. You can't just hear it and go on with your normal life; you can't unlearn depravity."

I swallowed hard, unable to hold back the tears.

"Remember what the doctors told us after Brittany was born?"

"You couldn't have any more babies, that you'd be risking your life? I thought it was all because of Brittany's size, that an infant that size really put a strain on you and your, umm, woman parts. It would be risking your life to have another child."

"Yes, I told you that," she smiled, amused. "And she was big! But my woman parts were damaged long before I became a woman. That's one of the reasons I love you so much. You don't ask questions; you just assume I have a good reason behind what I need or say."

"Yes," I said, thinking back. "If you—and they—wanted me to get a vasectomy, then I knew there had to be a good reason behind it."

"Well, they told me privately that it was a miracle that I delivered the girls, I was so scarred, so chopped up inside. I appreciated the fact that you never questioned why I was that way. You just accepted it, and went on from there." She paused, reaching for a deep breath. "I knew, because of our commitment to each other, that when I finally did tell you—maybe on that balcony overlooking the ocean at Hilton Head enjoying our retirement—that you would understand why I've been silent for all these years. And the difficulties I've had with intimacy."

"But now, I'm sick . . . sick to death, really." For a moment, she said nothing, and then continued. "But I also have a purpose beyond merely living through these weeks: to give you a chance to ultimately thrive after my passing. And get across to you just how serious, how committed I am to a fulfilled life for you and the girls." She tried to draw a breath, choked, and then tried again. I started to reach for the oxygen. She held up a hand. "Got this, I'm okay . . . or as okay as the beast in my body lets me be."

She closed her eyes, quickly diving into a sound sleep. I sat by her side, saying nothing and thinking nothing. Just sat. Finally, she spoke. "Faith in God, a personal relationship with his Spirit, and the all-encompassing wisdom of Ps 46 got me through all of this. And I'm still smiling. Not easily, my muscles are going, but still . . . smiling. And I want the same for you. The smiling, I mean."

Her fingers flattened on the rail. She closed her eyes. The room was still . . . "Be still and know that I am God!"

Minutes passed. And then slowly, carefully, Sharon fumbled her Bible from the bed beside her to her chest.

And opened it to Ps 46.

Charting a Course Driven by Spirit

Later, in the dark hours of early morning, after she had awakened, she said "What we're doing now is charting a course for your life after . . ."

"You're gone," I finished.

"I don't want secrets, sweetheart, I want honesty. I'm telling you all this . . . this . . . this sleaze, this horror because I want you to know how serious I am about you having a normal life, and getting beyond your grief. I also want you to help the girls get beyond their grief. That's important to me, the peace that will come with the assurance that you will change the way you think and live . . . for the better. *Stinkin' stuff*? *Psalm-46 it*. I want you to know how important Ps 46 has been throughout my life, allowing me to live a good life, fulfilled by the everyday blessings that God sends my way. You've been a blessing; the girls have been a blessing. My mom, a blessing. I want you to . . ."

She started choking again. I quickly put my hand between her back and the bed, and firmly moved her upright. At the same time, I flipped the switch on the machine that forced her to cough, positioned the mask on her mouth, and gently but firmly hit her back in time with the bursts of air. That produced a series of coughs that cleared her throat of the mucous before it could pool in her lungs. She no longer had the muscle capacity to clear her lungs unaided.

When she became more comfortable, I turned the machine off and lowered her to the bed.

"When I say 'Ps-46 it,' I'm asking you to stop, to be still, and let that supernatural link that God provides, his Spirit, help with your reaction to whatever issues, whatever *stinkin' stuff* you face. The first and worse for you and the girls: loss of a wife and mother, grief—huge, heavy, sit-on-your-chest grief. I want you to learn how to *Ps-46 it*, to apply Ps 46 to the challenges you'll face. *Psalm-46 it* to the bumps in the road, the issues and decisions. This psalm is both energizing and calming. It explains everything you need to know about being Spirit-led and Spirit-driven. It gives us strength and power in all circumstances—even those that may seem as insurmountable as those of a seven-year-old facing hell on earth.

"It may not change your physical circumstances; unfortunately, we're so much at the mercy of others, of situations we may or may not be complicit in making, of the health of our bodies, but it *will* change how you view those challenges. You *can* smile, you know, despite what you're facing. I'm smiling, as best I'm able, despite my disease. You *will* smile, despite your grief. Memorize this psalm, use it to give you wisdom and bravery and love, and you *will* move on from this terrible time"—she lifted her hand at the wrist, indicating the room filled with medical technology—"no matter. The verses surrounding verse 10 analogize life on this earth, what we often encounter. My condition, even. But God protects us amid the chaos of our lives, and gives us joy amidst the *stinkin' stuff* of disease and hate and disappointment and plain old bad breaks. He's that powerful, and he's there to protect, to serve us. We're his creation and he cares, he loves. He *is* love, he *is* caring and he got me through terrible times with that personal connection to his Spirit, established in the stillness."

Genuine Smiles

She gave a rasping chuckle. "Verse 10 is the key to connection, to tapping into his Spirit and being able to smile despite what life hits you with. It begins inside. Peace. Connection. Love. Smiles. Smiles are not just personal physical and emotional features. Smiles—genuine, as opposed to manipulative—are a sign that you're open to other views, other ways, a starting point for a flexibility that you'll need. You, especially, my dear contentious and often negative husband. You'll find that the world will be brighter once you let the Spirit of God guide you to a greater understanding of his word, to a more discerning and peaceful life."

"Psalm-46 It, ALS?"

"I have ALS, a terminal disease," she said flatly, "and all the health issues that go along with it. How do I live with it, right now, without being consumed by bitterness? How do we remain here for each other, despite the tragedy of this disease? By faith and liberal doses of Ps 46. God is with me every moment, every second, assuring me that there's something better waiting, and I need not fear. I suffer, yes; fear, no. ALS: *Psalm-46 it.*

"You're hurting," I said quietly.

"Yes. Very much so. Emotionally and physically. But truly, *'Be still and know'* changes my perception of what's next for me. Even as a little girl"—she gestured toward her midsection—"I reacted with hope through the stillness, convinced of his power. That I could *Ps-46 it*—without at first knowing that that was what I was doing—was a blessing, and continued to be more so when I figured out the enabling power of deliberately linking to him."

Her smile was slight and tired, but genuine.

Exhausted by the effort of talking, she closed her eyes and fell asleep.

I looked out the window. The snow had begun.

Doing What She Asked

I sat beside her bed that night, as I often did; thinking, trying to push back an anger that morphed into rage at what had been done to her. But there, beside the bed as she lay quietly breathing with the help of oxygen, I did what she asked: "Be still and know that I am God!"

Faith ran deep in Sharon, as did Ps 46, so much deeper than I had realized. If she could maintain her calm, knowing what she knows about ALS, experiencing the suffering that comes with its symptoms—well, I thought, I owe it to her to follow her lead. In all the years I had known her, she had displayed a remarkable peace, an ability to smile regardless of our circumstances. And now, I knew that that calm was something that had been developed throughout her life—*because* of her life—a peace that brought her power and the ability to rise above and beyond her circumstances.

Psalm-46 it. What you do to pain and hurt, to problems and challenges. And grief. May as well start now, with a year of dread having built to the bursting point. *Psalm-46 it*, and then let "Be still and know . . ." take me to where I need to be, where Sharon wants me to be. Let the Spirit lead, let him speak to me personally, internalize the "glorious works of God," the assurance that comes with the certainty that through the Spirit he "is our refuge and strength."

Psalm-46 it. Get to know the Spirit. May as well start now, I told myself. Nothing to lose but sadness and grief. And everything to gain—for me, our girls, and for future living and relationships.

The Meaning of Beauty

Those last months, especially the last weeks, were a series of deep dives into the faith of a woman who, because of her love for her family, bared her soul. She continually emphasized Ps 46, with its "magical and mystical and spiritual tenth verse"; the key to continuing life, love, and perseverance; a psalm that is "the power of God, Spirit, and faith explained in eleven verses."

Now I knew the source of her beauty, her calm, the sense of tranquility that had attracted me to Sharon and which she still possessed. The source: God's word, and Ps 46 in particular. She had always talked, had dressed, had moved with a grace reminiscent of times gone by, a classic beauty from a time when beauty was, indeed, classic. When beauty didn't come with nose rings and blue hair. When character wasn't dictated by social media, determined by video apps.

But more than beauty, she projected grace, even as she wasted away on a hospital bed in our middle room; a grace that comes directly from a God who loves and a lifetime of "Be still and know . . ."

As another great theologian (and singer), Rod Stewart, put it best in a hit song that has become a classic: "You wear it well, a little old-fashioned but that's all right."

Beauty Is as Beauty Does

"Physical characteristics are not beauty," she had said a number of times when we reminisced about our first meeting. She was front-and-center as a spokesperson for a premiere downtown Atlanta hotel, and continued modeling part-time after our marriage. "I've been around physical beauty as a model, and there's not a single beautiful woman that can hold a candle to a woman, regardless of physical appearance, through whom the grace of God shines."

Another characteristic, "a little old-fashioned but that's all right": She believed in shutting off the television, putting down the books and, later, the electronics, pushing away our work, and after our two daughters were asleep, spending at least an hour or so talking: About our daughters, our lives apart during my work travel; her busy mix of children, charities, and civic activities; about God and faith and spiritual connection, about doubts and fears, and always making sure that a hug and a kiss ended the day.

"'Be still and know,' applied to our everyday lives, means to be still and know your spouse, your children, your friends and coworkers. God speaks to us in the stillness, seeing what's on our hearts and in our minds. Especially when it comes to relationships of all kinds, in all places."

Psalm as Tuning Fork

Over the decades, I had come to understand, in a general way, that she had a special affinity for Ps 46, beginning with the tenth verse and cycling through the others and the Bible as the challenges of her life demanded. Psalm 46, beginning with stillness. This last held power for her, spiritual power and was the gateway to the discernment and peace available to us from all of Ps 46 and, indeed, all of God's word. In addition to providing a spiritual gateway, Psalm 46 establishes the parameters of a continuing talk—prayer—with God beginning with stillness.

"Stillness is a tuning fork that aligns us with God through the Spirit," Sharon said. "It brings us into oneness with his strength, comfort, and discernment. God is refuge, God is strength, and knowledge of God is the power to work through and above the ordinary ups-and-downs of our lives." She lifted her chin, smiling ironically. "And God knows, I need all of it. Anyway, that's my story and I'm sticking to it."

"Got it," I said.

"'Be still and know that I am God' is mystical, spiritual," Sharon explained, and Ps 46 is a very special and calming message, going beyond the ordinary choices made in life (which of us shuttles the girls to horseback riding lessons, who will take them to dance, feed the cats, put away the dishes?) to seek a spiritual connection that connects to a wisdom and surefootedness that allows us to cope with both the ordinary and the extraordinary events of life

"It doesn't just have meaning for your mind, your soul. It is *useful*, you can use it. It's why we worship—it helps us on a very personal level. I mean, why praise God, why worship him unless it makes us feel good, feel fulfilled, and able to thrive? Even now . . ."

"I'm so sorry," I interrupted, shaking my head in sorrow.

"Don't be," she said. "I accept where I am, what the doctors say I am."

The Spirit Plays Tennis

The tenth verse, she explained, is the start of a rewarding and direct relationship with the Spirit of God. It was that way for her and "for you as you deal with the grief of my passing."

"Talk to the Spirit, God," she urged. "Go back-and-forth in the stillness, out loud or in your head. That's prayer. Prayer may be short—one word, for example, 'help'—or long, a day spent on your knees."

"'Be still and know that I am God,'" she said, "is another way of saying 'pray, pray and listen all the time.' Old, New Testaments—same God, same message: Never stop praying. Be thankful in all circumstances."

"Paul," I commented.

She smiled wide. "A Jew, part of the spiritual aristocracy of the time. More kosher than a bagel with a schmear. Just like Jesus, another Jew, who we are certain knew the Old Testament like the back of his hand—or like the temple scrolls. Old or New Testaments, it all has one goal in mind: 'to do what is right, love mercy, and to walk humbly with your God.'"

I was used to her jumping in and out of the Old and New Testaments. "More Bible stuff."

"God stuff, Micah," she replied. "One of God's many messengers and a key to my life, our love, and now especially, our perseverance. Jewish—your background—or Christian, my upbringing. Psalm 46 is an invitation to submerge yourself, through awareness and prayer, in God's wonder: 'Come, see the glorious works of the Lord.' For me, now, his glorious works include getting through this, this *stinkin' stuff* of disease, and someday coming out the other side—for me, with him and what he's put together for life after life; for you, here in this world—whole and happy. The promise of God; the details courtesy of Jesus."

She paused. "See? Old to New and back again. Prayer as tennis match. Two books, one God. God, through Moses and the Spirit to me personally; Moses for the message—the Shema in Deuteronomy—and the Spirit for the personal meaning. 'Listen, O Israel! The Lord is our God, the Lord alone. And you must love the Lord your God with all your heart, all your soul and all your strength. And you must commit yourselves wholeheartedly to these commands that I am giving you today.'

"God wants me to keep going, keep living and loving—despite this disease, the beast in my body. Psalm 46: 'God is our refuge and strength, always ready to help in times of trouble.'"

"You're amazing," I said.

She took a deep breath. "Got to get in as much air as I can, while I can," she said with a wry smile, and then pointed to the surrounding mountains. "There's his beauty, his wonder, a reminder that 'When I am weak, then I am strong.'"

"Back to the New Testament," I said. "Got it."

She nodded, patting the Bible by her side. "Corinthians. Paul. All coming at me out of the stillness back there, in front of the hospital. The message: Keep on going, persevere. The road's going to get tough, but perseverance flowing from that stillness gets us through."

"Us?"

She gave a soft chuckle. "We're in this together, love. We both need perseverance, as '. . . the two are united into one.'"

"Another God-through-the-Spirit thing?"

"Genesis. The beginning of it all."

Perseverance

There was that word again: Perseverance. Later in the year, especially, when we had lived so much of our lives in the single room devoted to her care, we tapped the strength of the Lord—each in our own way—to deal with the progress of her disease. Perseverance: she, throughout the day in prayer, asking God to give her the strength to remain upbeat; me, struggling to stay awake in the chair beside her bed, working to remain positive and supportive.

"Strength," she said reflectively. She turned to me as the winter wind blew off the mountains and against the car after another UVA visit. "We'll need it—both of us. In different ways. I'm dying. There's no escaping it. And so, I'll live this next year, and you'll live this and many years after I'm gone."

She smiled again. The silence in the car was deafening until Sharon quietly quoted, in a voice both sad and hopeful, "'Pay attention to this, Job. Stop and consider the wonderful miracles of God!'"

She turned to me. "The book of Job."

"Bible stuff, huh?"

"Yes," she softly chuckled. "And God stuff. That's what came to me out of the quiet just now, 'Be still and know that I am God!' God is amazing. Out of the stillness came the reminder that God said to an unhappy but still faithful Job, and is now saying to me, 'Don't dwell on your tragedy. Instead look around, appreciate the beauty of this world, of what you *do* have. You have a husband, you have two daughters, all of whom love and will support you. The course of the disease—a done deal. Now is the time to stay strong, stay loving and kind and testify to what I've done in your life.'"

The diagnosis had settled her mind. At least she *knew*, we *knew*, the uncertainty of dark imaginings as her physical condition deteriorated behind us.

There was something about faith and spiritual connection, established by the stillness of what she called her "alone time with God," that pushed her to a different level of living and talking and now, passing . . . aka dying.

"Looking back over our years together, I took your peace, your equilibrium for granted. No matter the challenge, no matter the *stinkin' stuff*, Sharon would be unruffled. how did you ever do it?"

"When in doubt," she replied. "When in trouble, when there's turmoil—embrace God. Be still, connect and draw strength; and keep walking, keep smiling. If I can still smile, so can you."

7

Déjà Vu All Over Again

Déjà Vu All Over Again

IN THE DAYS AFTER Christmas, Sharon emphasized over and over that linking to the Spirit is a process and discipline, a way of connecting yourself to "a beyond-natural world of power and wisdom and joy." The more the disease progressed, the more determined she was to communicate the calm and joy underlying her life "so that you and the girls can understand and apply what's kept me going all these years . . . and even now."

"If I sound like I'm repeating myself," she finished, "it's because I am!"

"Sounds like Yogi Berra, 'It's déjà vu all over again.'"

She chuckled. "See? You can still get a smile out of me! After all these years, after all this *stinkin' stuff*—even now." Again, the fingers tapped for emphasis. "Now listen. Memorize and use Ps 46—it will get you through whatever you're facing, and it will also lead you to the rest of God's word." The fingers stilled. "And from that, my dear, dear husband, you'll find a continuing source of strength. God's word is Jesus, and Jesus is God's word. He's all one God; the Jewish God is the Christian God is the God of us all, and the path to strength, to peace in all circumstances, is through a personal relationship with his Spirit. Psalm 46 is God's word, and Jesus is there, if you're open to it; yes, déjà vu all over again. When you're in need, go to Ps 46, which also connects you to God in all his facets, to his one-ness and, yet, separateness according to your need for him. When you're in need, 'come to me and drink. Rivers of living water will flow from his heart.' The way of a personal Spirit, of God's word as useful, the way of meeting challenges and solving problems, of personal connection to and through the Spirit."

"More God stuff, I assume. Living waters is Spirit, right?"

She nodded slightly. "New Testament, John. A Jew, like Jesus. Like you. See? It's all connected, all part of a divine energy that helps you through this world. For me, it began with Ps 46, and continues. It's a set of words that is a way into all of the word, the sixty-six books of the Bible, a single voice and set of values. That voice has beyond-natural impact, with words that can produce the peace that I have laying in this bed, that will free you from debilitating grief, is Ps 46. So," she continued, looking at the indistinct light from the streetlamp coming through the window. "Psalm 46 when you have . . .

"Ordinary bumps in the road? *Psalm-46 it.*

"Horrendous circumstances? *Psalm-46 it.*

"Personal decision to make, need guidance? *Psalm-46 it.*

"I'm talking about all of this so that you'll understand that developing a relationship with the Spirit, with God, is critical to confronting both ordinary and extraordinary situations, to coming out the other end of tragedy with peace and a smile.

"I love you," she said, her eyes meeting mine, "and I want you to work through the grief of this ALS stuff by harnessing the strength, comfort, and power of the God of Ps 46."

She paused. "And, eventually, all of his word, the Bible. Be diligent, be disciplined, and you will eventually be led to other parts of his word." God's strength, joy, and wisdom, she continued, is "yours for the price of faith, of belief in the one God and the ability to connect to him through stillness. In that stillness, verse 10, you must have the discipline to slow down—however briefly, momentarily even, once you've become accomplished at establishing a connection—and let him speak to your heart, your soul. Slow down, pause, let thoughts and feelings and direction flow from the Spirit, your personal connection."

ALS, Dysfunction, and Pain

Do this enough, she said from her bed, and you'll have constructed a more joyful and discerning way to live. "Even while in intense grief. Memorize Ps 46. Meditate on it. Pray through it. And apply it.

"Think of it as a *Way*, not just a way. A path that slows you down, calms you, allows you to ignore, the best you can, the dysfunction inside."

"Dysfunction?"

"For some, inner rage; for others, the pain produced by traumatic experiences; and still others, rampant cynicism. There are so many dysfunctions. To be human is to experience dysfunction." She brought her fingers off the bed and moved them, indicating her body. "For me, now, the knowledge and pain of a terminal disease—physical dysfunction. Trauma of sorrow—mental dysfunction."

She paused for a breath, which grew shallower with each day passing. "Take every part of Psalm 46 as personal. 'Heaven's Armies' are here to support you. The stillness connection establishes his indwelling wisdom and strength. Believe in God, in his Spirit, in his ability to get you through your grief and whatever situations and other circumstances you face. Like ALS. Like grief. Face a situation and then *Ps-46 it*. Take in and apply the rock-solid faith that the psalm represents, its description of God as the source of strength, the Spirit as a way to link to God's power and love, and you'll experience a calm and peace you've never before had."

"I get it," I said. "Our conversations have established that, but it's hard to do it."

"I understand. But still . . ." She paused. "Try. Ask yourself: How can she lay here, with ALS, knowing what's coming, and not be a depressed mess? The answer: God. Spiritual linkage. Psalm 46. The power of the beyond-natural. Without him I'd never make it." She turned her eyes toward me and smiled slightly. "In truth, part of me is in fact a depressed mess. I mean, I have ALS and I will not live much longer and before I go, I *will* suffer, even more so than now.

"That's the whisper of a little voice inside, reminding of what's ahead. But faith and Spirit allows me to lower the volume of that voice, knowing that even with ALS, even with your grief both now and later, we 'cannot be destroyed. From the very break of day, God will protect' us. I will not panic. You will always have grief, but eventually it will be a grief composed of memories and love. Not gut-wrenching, paralyzing grief."

"But . . ."

Bill Shakespeare Puts His Two Cents In

She lifted a finger from the bed, easier at this point in the disease than raising her hand. "I know what you're thinking. We've been together too long for me not to know what you're thinking. 'But you have ALS. Some protection! Some God!'"

Her finger fell back to the bed. Just lifting it exhausted her. "And yet, I love him, I have faith in him, I know he's there, and I've treasured a lifetime of connection and advice. He created a universe where natural and beyond-natural principles govern the cosmos. Problems, stuff—*stinkin' stuff*—are part of both nature and humanity. That's built into the design—but that's theology and would take longer to discuss than I have left. And, ultimately the answer will come down to: 'Dunno.' So, I choose not to think about it because it just gets too . . . too complicated. Or, as Hamlet said to his friend, Horatio, 'There are more things in Heaven and Earth, Horatio, than are dreamt of in your philosophy.'"

I laughed. "Love it! Looks like God's word influences all that we do! Start with Ps 46, and follow the road to Yogi Berra . . . and Shakespeare, right? See, I remember my Cliff's Notes."

She gave my hand a reassuring pat. "God's there for us, through all of our world, through life and literature and even baseball, as boring as it's become. I don't have time to worry about 'how,' and neither do you—just accept that the results of memorizing and applying, with gratitude always, Ps 46 will produce miracles, large and small and all points between, in your life after . . ."

"You're gone," I finished.

"See," she said. "A bit of tearing up, but not much more. We're not crying, maybe a touch of sadness. But just a touch. Even now, here in this bed in this room in our house, I am grateful for the blessings I've enjoyed. And I'm grateful for the strength and wisdom that a personal relationship with the Spirit has given me to navigate the *stinkin'* patches, sometimes not patches but downright deserts of my life. He protects by giving me strength and purpose, and—when the actions of others break through the peace, the *shalom*—the ability to take whatever this world is throwing at me. Faith offers understanding and wisdom sometimes, but perseverance always. I want the same for you."

I sighed. Again. And again. I'd been doing a lot of that lately.

She gazed at me. "Now, you're my purpose, you're my legacy. The girls, too."

"But the girls aren't here, listening. You're only talking with me."

"They're grieving. They're hurt. I understand. But I'm going to reach them through you, later and in increments, by what you do with them, by what you say, how you continue—through your life—to *dad* them."

I laughed. "*Dad* them? You've turned it into a verb."

"Because it is. You will *dad* them, and they will work through the grief and find joy again. And joy for me will continue to and through the end, as long as I'm convinced that you're prepared to deal with the grief of my passing." She rotated a finger, indicating the room. "It's not a jumping around joy; it's the joy that comes from knowing, no matter what, that I'm accomplishing something during these last days. It's the joy of a personal relationship with God through his Spirit with you and through you the girls. And, not coincidentally, it's the joy of knowing that he's there for me now, as I tiptoe up to my last breath, and forever after."

"Yup. I understand."

Christmas Every Day Now

Thanksgiving and Christmas were behind us. The holidays had added both color and sadness to the household. At her insistence, I had put up our Christmas tree in the living room, decorated it, and turned on the lights the week after Thanksgiving.

"Let's keep the lights on beyond Christmas," she said. "All the time."

"When would you want the tree taken down?" I asked. Usually, we took our tree down the week after the New Year, but Sharon enjoyed watching from her wheelchair the ornaments twisting and reflecting in the light.

"You'll know when it's time," she said. "No dates. Leave it up as long as it feels right. That Christmas tree, with thirty years of ornaments, brings both of us joy . . . and this home can use some joy."

"Joy?" I drew a deep breath, then tried to be understated in my reaction. "Not what I'm feeling these days."

"I am," she said firmly. "A quietly melancholy joy. It starts inside with the conviction that no matter what, no matter what our circumstances, my illness and your grief, that all will be right for both of us. This disease is terrible. This disease stinks. This disease has brought a whole new and awful chapter to our lives. But we will get through and beyond this. And you *will* smile again."

"But joy?"

"Yes, joy," she said. "I'll pass and you will have grief. But you will gradually, over time, understand that life for you doesn't end at my grave. And you will discover a greater joy . . . if you listen to me . . . and allow Ps 46 and your spiritual relationships to permeate your life."

"Why talk like that?" I asked. "It's painful for you, and it's painful for me."

"I want you to understand that, just as the grave doesn't end my life, neither does your life end with my passing. ALS is terminal. Faith is forever. See where Ps 46 leads you; see what you're led to do, to feel in the stillness that begins with the tenth verse. There are no treatments that will prolong my life beyond the next month or so; thanks to the UVA clinics, I understand and accept that, all of that."

I nodded. Depth. This lady had depth. Amazing how you could know someone, be married to someone, and only skim in the shallows of that depth . . . because you let the busyness of ambition, career, and raising children fill your time and thoughts.

"Maybe in thirty years there will be a miracle cure, or extensive life-prolonging drugs. But not now. We can't affect the course of the disease. The feeding tube has meant that I won't starve to death, but that's all, really. Just a bit more comfort as my muscles atrophy. I know the muscles that control my breathing, my lungs, are dying. But with you and the girls I have purpose, here in this room, besides dying by millimeters. How do I deal with ALS? I have faith, and that faith has allowed me to find purpose. I like to think of you going on, getting through the grief, finding fulfillment, maybe even allowing yourself to experience the joy of relationship again. And only, once in a while, taking a glance in the rearview mirror; regrets, yes. Only natural. But no gazing in that mirror for long periods. Maybe enjoy a new relationship—if you choose—that's every bit as loving, but quite different from what we've had."

"No, no, please," I protested, holding up my hands. "That's not even something to think about. I mean, we have a beautiful Christmas tree. I'm here, you're here."

The Faith Connection

She nodded, her head lightly bobbing against the pillow. No matter what I said, she would be thinking about it—I recognized the nod. A we'll-let-it-be-for-now-but-don't-think-that's-the-end-of-it nod, followed by an I-know-something-you-don't-know smile.

How many times over our three decades together had I experienced that smile? And how many times had she been right? This last is a rhetorical question, of course; she had been right almost all the time, having a wisdom that, I now knew, came from the connection that deep faith brought to her life and a steadfastness that, no matter what, all would turn out well. What she knew that I didn't know, but she was determined to leave me with as a last gift, the power of a single song, read as poetry, from the Old Testament.

"Psalm 46 has been there for me throughout my life. It's hard to be poor, and it's hard to be a woman, and it's hard to be powerless. My mom was that all of her life: A single mom, rural West Virginia, no connections, no family traditions. Subsistence living. Work and me. Work and me, her only child. No drugs, though, not in our house. I started out with no power, no connections, no guidance, and no traditions.

"My mom did a great job and, despite what happened to me, I went on to be a cheerleader, enjoyed high school, even was a lead cheerleader, and lived a somewhat normal life. Didn't date, though; I tried it once and my stomach just churned—a direct result of what I went through. Patience, I thought, normalcy will come.

"Mom helped by being a wonderful mom. She taught cleanliness, discipline, and working hard to achieve your goals. We didn't have much, but we had clean floors and laundry, civility, ritual, and talk, lots of talk instead of watching television. I learned to be not only a mature adult, but a strong woman in that house. Great foundation."

"She did right by you."

A tear slowly made its way down her cheek. "Yes, she did. And she gave me the freedom to go beyond that foundation. As much as I was her life, she selflessly urged me to go to secretarial school for six weeks away from home when I graduated high school. She knew that I had developed faith and consequently rock-solid assurance. I've gotten through all of the challenges, all of the ugliness with a connection that has kept me from despair, encouraged me, helped me to realize connecting to God's Spirit is both process and conviction, accompanied by the ability to face whatever life on this world throws at you." Her eyes, sparkling through the tears, pierced the dimness of the room. "Like ALS.

"Memorize it, sweetheart, take Ps 46 into your heart as I have, and your life will change. That I can promise. You can get through this, stronger and more assured, no matter what these last days are like. Just listen to me, and practice. Practice. Psalm 46. Practice applying the psalm to your life; *Ps-46 it*, every problem, every roadblock, every decision, every time you enter this room and forever after.

"Practice Spirit, Practice faith. Practice God." She gently smiled.

Master of Dumb

She spent much of her time sleeping. But each night I'd lift her into a wheelchair, pull the strap snugly around her chest, and push her to view the lights on the Christmas tree in the living room. I sat quietly next to her on a chair. We were alone in the house.

The lights played across her face. "I'm going to tell you some more about me, about some things we never talked about. I'm doing this so that you can understand how Ps 46 got me through some terrible moments, some terrible times. And I'm doing this so that I will have an impact beyond our last conversations, so that you'll have this ability to apply the psalm imprinted on your heart."

I shook my head as we watched the lights twinkle off the ornaments. "I know everything I need to know. You've been the best wife . . . ever! You've been the best mom to our girls . . . ever! I know you've loved all of us, no matter what stupid things we've done, no matter what trials we've put you through. I'm including myself in that. Looking back, at times I've been the master of dumb."

She smiled, the lights reflecting off her face. "Yes, in many ways, you have been."

"Gee, thanks. You know, I was just trying to be humble."

Now her eyes were laughing. ALS, yes; laughter, still yes. "Psalm 46 won't save you from every misstep, every natural and manmade disaster. It sure didn't save me. But it will give you the confidence, assurance, and perseverance to get through them. You have to intentionally apply it, seeking wisdom and guidance. The Spirit can only work with what he's got, what you give him. He can't immediately cure dumb, but he can help you endure the consequences. And the Spirit can help you learn from your mistakes, your wrong decisions."

Faith, Strength, and Accepting Reality

Throughout the night, she periodically struggled awake to recount the story of another part of her past—again, who knew?—to emphasize her faith and perseverance amidst trauma and unwise decisions. In the late sixties, a decade before we met, she had stepped penniless from a Greyhound bus in Atlanta. She had finished the six-week stint at a secretarial school in Washington, DC, where she stayed with relatives and took a city bus to class. Secretary was presented as the sinecure for a female from a poor household graduating from a rural West Virginia high school. The instructors at the secretarial school, who taught her to type and take dictation, told her that secretarial jobs were abundant in that booming southern city. So off she went, with her mother's blessing.

She knew no one, on her own in a city fourteen hundred times as large as her tiny hometown. She bravely clutched her cardboard suitcase, put her God connection into gear, and smiled at the new world around her. After paying for a bus ticket, she had just enough money left to buy a snack and a newspaper to scan the classified advertisements for lodging. She was fortunate, however; she walked deliberately through the drug addicts and pimps inhabiting the downtown Atlanta bus station and asked a police officer advice on the safest and least expensive women's hostels that were also on a bus route. He directed her out of the urban blight to safety. She walked more than seven miles that first day in search of the lodging suggested by the officer. No taxi. Just walking.

"We've never talked about it," I commented. "You are an amazingly strong person."

"I *was*—and *am*—what I need to be to make life work. Through God's guidance I found the hostel for women. Was I scared when I stepped off that bus, all alone in a downtown Atlanta bus terminal? You bet! Did I stand in the middle of that station, close my eyes, ignore the predators and junkies, and recite to myself Ps 46? Yes, and that's when I found a friendly police officer. Then, after walking all day, through God's grace, I located the hostel for women. *Psalm-46 it*—I had a safe place to stay while looking for a job."

She found a job immediately in the headquarters of a railroad. Her instructors had been right; Atlanta was fertile ground for skilled secretaries. With her new salary, she was soon able to move out of the hostel and rent a one-bedroom apartment . . . and meet the musician who would be her first husband.

8

Rape . . . and Hope

Sometimes You Just Make Dumb Decisions

I LIFTED HER FROM the bed, placed her in the wheelchair, and slowly pushed her to the living room, where we enjoyed the Christmas lights reflecting from the ornaments, a reminder that Sharon, for all of the time I'd known her, had faith and thereby God.

"Sometimes I'm surprised by having made it this far," she said. "But faith tells me that, with God, 'all things are possible.' Even surviving my first—and awful—marriage."

I nodded. "More God stuff."

"Good God stuff, encouraging God stuff. The gospel in the New Testament ties right into 'God's voice thunders, and the earth melts!' And so many other parts of the Old and New Testaments. See? New, to Old, to New, and back again!

"I was eighteen years old when we married. He was more than a decade older. I had stopped in a bar with a friend after work. There he was, playing his guitar on the stage in the front of the room, so glamorous, playing Atlanta clubs three or four nights a week. He didn't have much of a voice, but it didn't matter; I was young, from rural West Virginia and he was glamorous. When he sang and looked directly at me, I fell in love. I was just a secretary.

That was a time when administrative assistants were not adminis-trative assistants, 'just' secretaries, all of us women and all second-class in large corporations. I was 'just' a secretary, in my teens, and here in Atlanta was this real musician in a real club, singing to me. Talk about flattered! How could I not end up with him? How could I not marry him?"

I lifted my eyebrows, a half-smile on my face.

"I know, I know," she said. "Foolish. Dumb. But being young means being foolish, wherever you're from. And that's the thing about prayer: Sometimes you just don't stop to think, you im-merse yourself in the stillness and you don't really listen. I had not yet built the discipline that I needed to run every decision by the Spirit; I was immature and naive, both in life and in Spirit, and should have let God talk. I just did not yet have that discernment I'd grow into in later years.

"And being a young, naive woman? I was surprised by how flattered I felt, how validated. This older man was paying attention to me. This mature older man. My dad died when I was two years old; the only experience of him came through my mother, who used to tell me that, if he had lived, she probably would have killed him. He was a drinker, hitting bars after work before staggering home late at night to fall into bed. That was his Irish heritage, she later told me. Irish, that was his excuse, or so my mom told me. He liked to drink, fight, and argue. Family? His little girl? Not so much.

"Not the best start to life," I said. "I'm surprised you even married."

Music and Marijuana

"He was not just a boyfriend; he was a father figure, I suppose, a musician who seemed larger than life, and I was flattered by the attention. No, beyond flattered. So, we married. Our wedding was a court clerk, followed by music and marijuana—on his part, not mine . . . mom wouldn't have approved. He and his friends, drunk in our apartment living room. Most of my savings went for the apartment, the rest for the party. All his friends seemed to be drunks and potheads. He continued playing clubs while giving the occasional guitar lesson on the side, barely eking out a living. He spent what little he made on beer and marijuana. But my income, at least ten times what he was bringing in, allowed us to move after we married to a larger apartment in a nicer area of Atlanta. And my salary bought everything outside of strings for his guitar and marijuana. I just refused to pay for that."

"Regrets?" I asked.

"Almost immediately. I had this idea that we would save our money, get a pretty home in the suburbs, and have a family. He would be Mr. Cool working his way up to larger venues, and Mr. Loving, coming home to me and our children at night. And we would evolve into *Leave It To Beaver* and *Father Knows Best*, Musician-Cool Edition."

"Nothing wrong with wishing and hoping," I commented.

"That's all it was, wishing and hoping. That my situation would improve. That he would want enjoy settling down with me, his wife. That he would grow into a family. But it didn't happen. He slept into early afternoon every day, got up, drank beer, and smoked some weed. When he wasn't working—which was most nights—he'd go out, meet his friends at a bar or club, and bring them all home at closing time. Smelly, trash-talking people jammed into our living room, fouling up our bathroom, breaking our furniture. Where'd he get the money for his life of leisure, his carousing? Me. We had the best apartment of the lot of them, and all because this just-a-secretary worked hard and brought home a more than decent salary. It was a miserable marriage; I had really thought he wanted what I wanted, a family and love. I thought he shared my dreams."

"Because?"

"Because he told me so. Didn't he sing the dream the first time he laid eyes on me? Wasn't he incredibly romantic, speaking directly to my teenage soul when he sang 'If I were a carpenter, and you were a lady . . . I give you my onliness. Give me your tomorrow.' It was a real-life fairy tale coming true. Little did I know that was his standard pickup song in the bars he played in. He was spreading around a lot of 'onliness,' and I was foolish enough to think his 'onliness' was just for me. On any given night you could find at least a half-dozen recipients of his 'onliness' in our living room."

"You had a dream. Family, children, nice home—I can see that."

"Children, of course, the dream of an only child. Each with brothers and sisters. And I knew that's what he wanted because he also sang, 'If I were a carpenter, and you were a lady . . . Would you marry me anyway? Would you have my baby?' I was dumb, I know."

"No," I said. "You were nineteen. You were sweet, inexperienced, a hillbilly girl susceptible to big-city liars and fakes."

She looked at the Christmas tree, lost in thought. Then she turned to me, "I'm ready for bed. Enough time in this wheelchair."

Rape

Back in her room, Sharon turned her eyes to the winter outside the window. I settled into our conversation chair.

"He was an aging hippie, who cared only for himself. A narcissist. I didn't want to see that. Unfortunately, I let myself be used. I financially supported him and that unwashed, lazy crowd that he brought into the apartment just about every night. It was the time of free love, right? That wasn't in my fantasy, dirty people drifting in and out, eating me out of house and home, smoking dope and having sex. On the couches I had paid for. On the carpeted floor that I was paying for. Marriage? 'Hey, man,'" she said in a mocking manner, imitating a hippie. "'What's that?' Our marriage was the magic of food appearing in our fridge every day, jam sessions and booze and sex into the wee hours of the morning while I slept alone in our back bedroom because I worked every day and needed my sleep. I worked normal hours and paid for a nice apartment that, to his way of thinking, automatically got cleaned and the food replenished when I came home from work. I was beyond foolish. And I was used."

I shook my head. "You were young and naive, that's all."

The tears glistened. "Every night I'd go down the hall to our bedroom, going to sleep early while they partied. Our apartment door was always open, with people from the clubs drifting in and out. He'd usually fall asleep on the couch or floor when the booze and drugs kicked in." She looked at me. "I wanted *Father Knows Best* in a husband. But he was definitely not *Father Knows Best*, and he was no Jim Anderson."

Jim Anderson, the wise and humble father in the television show, *Father Knows Best*. Gentle, loving, and kind; wonderful father and husband. I sniffed, and said, "No, not Jim Anderson."

She smiled sadly. "And one night *Father Knows Best* collided with reality. Which, in retrospect, was more *Mad Max*."

I nodded. "The movie about a post-nuclear war dystopia. Harsh, not hippie."

"Harsh, hateful, vicious, depraved. Uncompromising and impossible-to-overlook reality. In the back of my mind, I remember the lighted face of the alarm clock by my bed, 3:30 a.m., just a flash forever seared into my memory because I awoke to find someone on top of me. One of the 'friends,' part of the stream of filth people flowing through my apartment. I struggled to get up but he forced me back down on the bed, his palm covering my mouth. So much I don't remember.

"But it's there, deep in my head, half-lit images in the dim green of the alarm clock. The bass from the other room thumping in the background. He lifted his hand and slammed his forearm into my throat. The other hand went across my mouth. I fought to free myself, fought to breathe. Sometimes I caught a breath, sometimes I didn't. The struggle for air, his weight, his arm crushing me. The smell of alcohol and marijuana and body odor gagged me."

She closed her eyes. "And then I was raped."

"Raped?" I shook my head in horror. "I didn't know about that! I wish I knew."

She opened her eyes, which were seeing beyond the room, back in the past. She continued. "No reason to tell you, just something I chose to forget as best I could. But you never forget, of course, Just like when I was a seven-year-old, I didn't want those images, that experience at home, and now I don't want it in our marriage. Besides, that kind of thing was completely beyond your experience. I didn't want you to even think about it."

She paused, then continued. "'Keep quiet or I'll slit your throat.' 'Don't move, bitch!' I remember 'slit your throat.' I remember 'bitch.' I remember thinking, no. No, no, no, no, no.

"I remember . . ." She trailed off. The silence hung heavy in the room. "I tried to scream, but it stayed inside my head as he increased the pressure on my throat, my mouth. He took the hand from my throat and pulled up my nightgown. The screams were silent, and kept echoing inside my head: This isn't happening; it was my apartment; I paid for it. How can this happen? I remember a knife, I remember the threat, I remember the smell; the utter terror and helplessness and pain and panic, the hell my life had become. And I still remember the pain, both physical and mental, and the feeling of total hopelessness."

I was speechless.

"When he had finished and slipped out of the room, back down the hall to *my* living room and the bodies passed out on *my* couches, the emptied beer cans that had started out in *my* fridge, the drug paraphernalia scattered across *my* furniture and *my* rugs, I staggered to the bathroom, locked the door, stepped into the shower, and washed in the dark . . . and washed and washed and washed. And then washed some more. And cried and cried and cried. And cried some more. And, finally, no more tears. I looked at the girl in bathroom mirror, in the gloom of the lights filtering through the steam on the window from the street lamps outside, and she looked horrible. Terrible. Used. Broken."

A faraway look crept into her eyes. She had left the room, this room. "God, where are you?"

In the background, the hiss and hum of the bed rollers, massaging her increasingly lifeless body, helping to prevent bed sores.

Newfound Strength

And now she returned. "But I wasn't broken. I closed my eyes, standing there. 'Be still and know that I am God,' the tenth verse plucked from Ps 46. The terror and pain slowly subsided. I recited the entirety of Ps 46 to the girl in the mirror. Something whispered inside, something that let me know I was not alone, that God dwells in me, that I 'will not fear when earthquakes come and the mountains crumble into the sea,' and then I knew the marriage was over. 'He breaks the bow and snaps the spear; he burns the shields with fire.'

"My marriage: As broken as my body, my mind at that moment. My marriage commitment: Snapped and burned. Now, I was free. New thoughts came into my mind. All of this was over. Somewhere deep inside, an inner voice was urging me on, encouraging me. I would not live in hell. I would not be used anymore. I would no longer be passive, something that the culture and my own inclinations pushed me into being."

"Newfound strength," I whispered, quiet and low.

"Sometimes you have to walk through the fire to get to the other side."

"Bible stuff," I murmured, the words catching in my throat.

A bare nod. "I learned early, in school, and from the people around me, that being passive was expected and my future was limited by my gender."

"But you defied the stereotypes and went your own way."

"Yes, in this and as in all of my life up to this point and after, God was there to guide me. I connected to the Spirit through the stillness of Ps 46, and found strength in the power of God, the knowledge that although 'the oceans roar and foam,' the Spirit will always be there for me."

"Even after rape?"

"Especially after rape. I cleaned up, put on my clothes for work, and packed a bag, just a few things; picked my way through the drugged-out bodies sprawled in the living room; and walked to my car. I drove to a diner and drank coffee until it was time for work. I spent my lunch hour looking at apartments for rent, and at the end of the day, after work, moved into a tiny apartment about five miles from where we lived, leaving him and his apartment and his music and filth behind. I wouldn't pay another cent in rent for him, no more groceries, no more beer. And time for him to buy a car. My car went with me—let him get his own car. He now owned his life, including our failed marriage. That was the guidance I received from the Spirit, God's direct line into my soul, my heart."

"You didn't call the police?"

"That just wasn't me. It was a lot of work in those days to establish rape, even if the police—largely male—believed me. And that wasn't a 'given.' The tendency was—and is—to blame the woman." A wisp of a wry smile. "I am and remain a woman."

"True," I smiled.

"And as a woman, there are so many built-in prejudices you have to deal with, especially in the south, and I didn't want go through that at that point. Yes, we're enlightened, more so than the rest of the world, but still, we've a long way to go. My struggle was personal, and I did what I could, given who and where and when I was. Something told me, deep inside, that the best approach was to quietly leave and put everything behind me. Now. Right away. Sever ties, which means divorce. Let him figure out how to get a car, how to pay for the apartment, how to put food in the refrigerator and clean up after his crew." She snorted. "Or not: Cleanliness was simply not a part of his lifestyle, of their lifestyle."

Don't Look Back

"Once you were out of there . . ."

"I didn't look back. Yes, I took the necessary steps to get an official divorce, but that I viewed as a here and now legal document. Be still, breathe deeply, and let the Spirit permeate your mind, your body. Then, do what you're led to do in any given situation. Start from where you are, then go to there. Walk, steadily and with assurance. Find a way to smile again, because although all around you may be chaos—'"

"So, you were led to build a new life, quietly and with a minimum of fuss, and put what happened out of your mind?"

"Yes, but . . . I was changed by all of that, I was different. No more meekly putting up with what had become the hell of our life together. But . . . my approach, the one I worked out in the silence of that bathroom, was to simply gather up my things and leave." She looked at me. "You know what they say: You break it, you own it. His life, his wreck of a marriage, his tawdry lifestyle; he owned it. I went on to a better life that included you and the girls. And I've never looked back. The Spirit gave me the strength to do that."

The Aftermath: Strength and Peace

"I wish I had known."

She shrugged, her ravaged muscles struggling to lift her shoulders. "It wouldn't have made a difference to us. I had intended to talk about it, when the time was right, but somehow the time never seemed right. We've had such a joyful life. Just like with the abuse—why bring it up?"

I nodded understanding, and she continued. "But now the time seems right. You need to know how serious I am about you finding a way to push the grief back, to go on with your life. If I can get through all of the *stinkin' stuff* I'm telling you about, then you can surely get through the grief of losing your best friend and marriage partner. *Psalm-46 it* and build a fulfilling and joyful life. Close your eyes, allow the peace to flow, push out the anxieties of life without me. You'll find peace amidst the pain of my passing. Remember, Ps 46 was always a part of my spiritual life, from the time I was seven years old, and right up to now."

"Peace," I nodded. "Problem, issue, crisis: *Ps-46 it*. But it doesn't change the reality of your death."

"No, but amidst the pain you can find peace, wisdom, discernment, and the ability to deal with the *stinkin' stuff* of life. I did. Maybe not successfully every time—that's life, right?—but Ps 46 gave me the strength to keep on walking. *Psalm-46 it* and you can feel the spiritual connection, the love and support and guidance.

My goal is for you to make the power of Ps 46 instinctive, something you do both on a conscious and subconscious level. When the grief overwhelms, *Ps-46 it*; when it seems like the cards are stacked against you, *Ps-46 it.*"

I sighed heavily.

"I guarantee. Memorize it, think about it, apply it. It all starts with 'Be still and know . . .' If I used it in that bathroom that night, after the rape—then you can apply it to grief. Memorize the psalm, sweetheart, and meet every challenge with 'Be still and know . . .'"

9

Abortion: Thank God for Forgiveness

O Christmas Tree

BY THE END OF December Sharon's core had weakened to where she couldn't sit upright in bed or the wheelchair without support. Her breathing was becoming increasingly labored. But we continued to end each day with two field trips in the house. Both involved God and faith.

"Little trips," she commented wryly, acknowledging that her life had been reduced to a series of small struggles. "But whole bunches of gratitude for the opportunity to get out of bed."

For the first, I would strap her into a wheelchair just before the winter sunset, and position her to view the wooded ravine overlooking the creek behind our home near the Blue Ridge Mountains, enjoying the stark and frosty beauty of the poplars, dogwoods, and oaks in the winter. Later, after she napped to recover strength lost in her previous outing, I again lifted and gently placed her in the wheelchair and rolled to the front room of the house, where the lights and ornaments of the Christmas tree provided ready cheer, now day and night, and especially elegant after dark. The tree was hung with ornaments commemorating the past thirty years as a family and our time together: souvenir ornaments from our vacations, the girls' handmade ornaments from their time attending Montessori; a flood of joyful memories.

Two to three weeks to go at the most on her internal clock, maybe a month she reminded me. The Christmas tree twinkled in front of us, reflecting off her increasingly gaunt face. But her eyes sparked with light. "The Lord of Heaven's Armies is here among us," she whispered, again turning to Ps 46. "The God of Israel . . ." Jacob, aka Israel, profoundly flawed, physically hurting after wrestling with God and riding an emotional roller-coaster for much of his life. ". . . Is our fortress," she finished. But God was there for him during an often-tumultuous existence. The lesson, Sharon's lesson, life through the lens of Ps 46 and faith: God will guide, God will protect, God will shield—both physically and emotionally. If you have faith, even "just a bit."

"Let there be light." Sharon managed a smile. "Bible stuff, as you like to say."

"God stuff, good stuff," I returned.

She managed a small smile, bright and wan at the same tie. "Not perfection, not utopia . . . just light. And all the blessings that flow from it. Just a bit, just a few—a bit of light, a few blessings. A few—that's all I need, all you need."

Dad Jokes . . . Supplied by God

"I've enjoyed my life, and our family. I love you and the girls, my mom. I don't love ALS, of course. I hate it." She gazed at the tree. "But there's nothing we can do about it. The best we can do is stay strong and stay together. Be part of God's 'fortress.' I'm ready for this last part, to let go. I'll pass . . . soon. Maybe even a week, but it doesn't feel like more than three weeks, maybe four."

She haltingly held up a trembling hand to forestall any attempt by me to wrap reality with soft words. "But I'll pass knowing that your lives will be better if I give you, and the girls through you, the ability to smile, to be positive, to go on with your lives. Your growing personal relationship with the Spirit will help them."

"But they're adults, grown up. They're on their own now, far away."

"You'll be surprised at how faith will change your outlook on life, bringing to you good thoughts, a continuing ability to pray, and the power to change relationships with the girls. I promise. God promises. Talk with him in the stillness."

"I should have done better with them, with you." Guilt and grief—that's what she foresaw, and, for the most part, forestalled.

"Sweetheart, you've been a great dad. A great dad exerts a lifetime of influence."

"And you've been an awesome mom."

She smiled. "Took the girls a while to recognize us as the awesome parents we are," she said with a twinkle in her eyes.

"Human nature," I replied, both of us still looking at the tree, sitting side by side, she in her wheelchair and me in an upholstered wingback.

"Yes, and now it's time for you to rise above that nature, that tendency in you—in all of us, really—to react without thinking. It's time to go that next step beyond awesome dad to a spiritual dad and individual, to make your faith truly useful in all situations. There's nothing more useful than God, than living faith. Believe me, the girls will feel that calm, that peace as they deal with the grief of my passing and continue the challenges of career and family. And they may, occasionally, turn to you for advice."

I snorted. "Not so sure about that!"

"I am. They'll see their father developing a sense of peace, of an inner wisdom that allows you to make the right moves." She smiled. "Your maturity may just keep up with your age . . . and elevate your jokes. Your dad jokes—always been awful."

"Hey! As those great theologians, The Three Stooges, put it, 'I resemble that remark!'"

"God may help you on that." Her eyes twinkled. "But whether he does or doesn't, you'll set an example by your ability to meet challenges, calmly and with a smile on your face, no matter what you're confronted with. Regardless of how you feel. Courtesy of a personal relationship with the Spirit."

"I suppose so," I said doubtfully, gazing at the tree.

Don't Go All Jewish on Me

Her eyes started to close. She quickly blinked them open. "Stick with me now on this. Faith and a personal spiritual connection are the bedrock of not just surviving, but thriving. Memorize Ps 46, be ready . . ."

"Again, with the Ps 46?!" I lightly chided her.

"You got it," she said, her smile widening. "So don't go all ethnic Jewish on me with that 'Again with the Ps 46?!'"

"Hey, leave my upbringing out of this," I joked.

She coughed out a laugh. "Your inflection—you sound like your mother. Be prepared to use all we've talked about, not just in crisis, hurt and pain, but when you have to make an important decision, or just want encouragement. And memorize the psalm in such a way that you can pluck the verses you need out of the beginning, the middle, or the end. But always begin with 'Be still and know.'"

She rested her hand on one of the scrapbooks she had put together over the years. She had asked me to put them on her lap, and we looked at them in the light of the tree. Our girls learning to ski; the sandcastles built at the beach; toddlers at Disneyworld; the two of us in Chicago for long weekends.

"So many wonderful memories." Her eyes were both sad and happy at the same time. "But Ps 46 will provide a path to different memories ahead for all of you. He will allow you to turn from grief to living your life with joy. Joy—that's faith, actually. God wants you to have joy after the grief, which is what I, too, want."

"I get it. You want me to be happy?"

"Yes, and I want you to be *joyful*, having the kind of joy we've had throughout our years together. Joy is deep," she rasped. "It's more elemental; it's a positive peace that speaks to your very soul—you know, the place that connects to the beyond-natural universe, through which the Spirit flows and guides.

"The same Spirit that I rely upon to get me through each day. I have joy, despite the ALS. I couldn't make it through this without that joy, which results from faith and a personal relationship with the Spirit. 'Be still and know' followed by 'that I am God!' He . . . or she, as it doesn't matter, because God is pronoun-proof—is one God, whether you view him through a Christian, Jewish, or perhaps an agnostic lens, and there for you through the link made easier by Ps 46 and its application, *Ps-46 it.*"

I nodded. "Not much left to say," I said, as we settled into companiable silence. "Except I love you."

"We're almost there," she whispered. "Psalm 46. You *will* overcome the turmoil of my passing, and find peace in the face of all the *stinkin'* stuff of life after . . ."

". . . 'I'm gone,' of course." I finished.

Rape? You Were Probably Asking for It!

A day later again in front of the Christmas tree. Our conversations took place in short bursts throughout the day and night, as she became increasingly unable to communicate without frequent naps. I would sit beside her for hours, often overnight; sometimes drifting off to sleep, other times watching the lights twinkle and reflect off of the ornaments, waiting for her to awake.

The New Year came and went.

"This may be my last time out here in front of the tree," she rasped. She was no longer able to keep her head up. I had adjusted the wheelchair to support her upper body and head, but she was increasingly limp, muscles no longer responding.

"No, no," I protested. "We'll have more."

"Maybe, but probably not. So let me get this out. More examples of relying on Ps 46. After I left my first husband . . ." She smiled as best she could. "You're my second . . . and my best."

"Low bar," I joked. I reached over and gently rubbed her hand. "But I'll take it."

She sighed and continued her story. "A short amount of time had passed and I filed for divorce."

"Smart move," I said. "Divorce is sometimes necessary."

"Yes, I had told him so many times about the life I had envisioned, about having a family. His usual reaction: a silent shrug, then back to the guitar. But this time, on the phone, calling him from my new apartment, it was different. I needed him to sign the divorce papers—otherwise, it would cost me more in time and money, both of which were in short supply, to go to court. In addition, I was feeling nauseous when I woke up in the mornings, and periodically throughout the day. Figured it was psychological. Made even thinking hard. Ultimately, I went to a clinic for a pregnancy test and, sure enough, the test was positive. I was pregnant. Was it him? Was it the rape? Based on the timing, I was certain it was the rape. I was in the process of divorcing him, and now a pregnancy. I let him know."

"What was his reaction?"

"Anger. At me. I told him by phone about the rape about two days after I left. I didn't know about the pregnancy until weeks later. But he didn't want to talk about what his 'friend' had done. Besides, he said—over the phone, of course, as I refused to go back to our apartment and he, a busy musician, had no interest in meeting me, his wife, in person elsewhere—said simply 'I don't believe it. Half the women in the places I play have screamed rape for one reason or another.'"

The festive lights of the tree seemed to dim under her intense gaze. "I paused. I thought my fist would crush the phone, that's how tight I was holding it. 'Maybe because they *have* been raped,' I answered, struggling to maintain my calm, my *shalom*, my peace. Be still and know, I summoned. The Spirit reassured: 'The Lord of Heaven's Armies' is here with you, your 'fortress,' I told myself."

"'You're no different,' he said coldly. 'So, I don't want to hear about it now. Anyway, if it happened, you were probably asking for it. Or you were just sleeping with one of my friends, for the pleasure of it.' I was horrified . . . and speechless. So nasty, so vile, so ice cold. I closed my eyes. 'Be still,' a soothing voice whispered. 'Listen to me. All around you is "in chaos" but their hold on you, the space they occupy in your mind, "will crumble."' Psalm 46.

Then, instinctively, my hold on the telephone relaxed. The rage, the hatred faded."

I stared at the Christmas tree, feeling the disgust, and fighting off anger.

All Women Sleep Around

"I was angry, hurt, and horrified, all at the same time. I'm a woman, and all women claim rape at some time or another, right?! All women sleep around when they have the opportunity? I was asking for it? My husband?! Really?! That was his response, which was in line with his views of women in general. But I wasn't a woman in general, an object; I was specific, an individual, and had been and still was—until the divorce was final—his wife. I had lived with him for almost five years, five years of trying to have a mutually committed and respectful relationship, and I remained a second-class citizen, no more than a supplier of, well, food and beer and sex. I thought I had escaped those kinds of misogynistic—a word I learned later—behaviors and attitudes when I left home, but it was evident that they were as much a part of the music and bar culture he was involved with in Atlanta as hillbilly West Virginia.

"That's the world we live and have lived in, especially forty years ago. I had tried, during that marriage, to establish an equal footing, but it's easy to forget that two people can see the same thing and think of it entirely differently. I had a secretarial job that paid well, I maintained our apartment and bought groceries, I paid for his living expenses—including a car—which allowed him to spend all his money on new guitars, beer, and marijuana. I rarely missed going to a club or bar to watch him sing; and, silly me, I thought for sure he appreciated it, and for sure we were of equal status. In the end: Of course, it's only natural you're supporting me, of course you're traipsing to the clubs with me; of course, we do things my way and never yours—you're my wife, and by definition a woman is less than a man."

Her eyes teared. "A bit of sarcasm there. My interpretation of what he thought. Five years wasted, I realized."

"When did you let him know you were divorcing him?"

"About three weeks after I left."

"He didn't contact you at all, asking where you were? Seriously?!"

By the Way, Your Friend Raped Me

She chuckled. "Seriously. I'm sure he speculated: Maybe I was with someone; maybe I went to visit my mom; maybe I was with friends. No curiosity. After all, he had his music, his friends, and the rent was paid through the month. He hadn't called after I fled our apartment; instead, 'Be still and know . . .' and I summoned the strength to call him. The first call: I'm done and, by the way, your friend raped me; the second call, I have an attorney and filed for divorce; the third, I'm pregnant. Funny thing was, not 'ha-ha' funny, that I was so conditioned to my role as a woman, a hopeful woman, that I had this little girl's hope that he'd say, 'Hey, come on back, I'm going to get cleaned up, won't make every night a party night, will work more, will take my commitment as your husband seriously. I'll change!' Dumb, very dumb. I should have hung up after letting him know it was over, and let my lawyer do the talking. But lawyers have meters running and charge with every letter, every phone call, and that was a consideration. Vivid memories: My fairytale thoughts of a happy ending were quickly shattered."

She closed her eyes and recited from memory:

> "Where do you expect me to get the money to live?" he demanded.
>
> "Work more," I retorted. "Not my problem. What about the rape? What are you going to do about it?"
>
> "I don't believe it," he said. "You're making it up, They're my friends."

I could feel the rage building. I wanted to go down to Atlanta and do something about it. But . . . I was forty years too late. So, I took a deep breath, used "Be still and know . . ." and a sense of calm settled upon me. And the realization that time travel was not one of the gifts of a personal relationship with the Spirit. Instead, I shook it off. Faith. I had learned. We were where we were, it is what it is, and I simply and lovingly offered, "I don't know what to say except . . . I love you."

She gazed at the tree. "Thanks, darling. There's nothing to say now. The purpose of telling you is not so that you can right the wrong, but to illustrate how the Ps 46 approach got me through a horrendous physical and emotional time in my life. And it can do the same for you."

"I don't understand how you can be so calm about it."

"The first thing I did on that phone was reach into and through in my mind, practicing stillness. It would do no good at this point getting visibly upset. I needed support and that's where a personal relationship with the Spirit comes in."

She stared at the tree. "Was I upset? Yes. Distraught? No. I knew there was no way to convince him otherwise, nor did I really want to. The divorce was already in progress and all I wanted was to be done."

Abortion as Blackmail

It was, in fact, her last time in front of the Christmas tree. Most of her muscles had atrophied now, and she had increasing trouble breathing and talking. I set up a small tree with lights on top of the bureau in her room, the only surface not covered by medical equipment. Our conversation continued, in fits and starts, taking place in brief moments throughout the nights and days.

"A few weeks later, I learned I was pregnant. I told him. 'Get an abortion,' he said, 'And I'll sign the divorce papers. But I'm not going to pay for any part of the divorce, and I'm not going to pay for an abortion—you're the one who got pregnant. Just leave me alone, let's get this over with. And unless you get an abortion, I'll fight the divorce. No abortion, no divorce.'"

"Lovely," I commented sarcastically.

"Sweetheart, I got everything done as quickly and quietly as possible. An easy divorce, uncontested, no alimony, no possessions, nothing to pay but the lawyer, an abortion that my mom and the lawyers and court knew nothing about." She sighed again and looked through the window, past the shrubbery, focusing on a street dim and gray under a partial December moon. Finally: "And always, I've wondered, what that child would be like. Over the years, I've regretted having the abortion, but I made the best decision I could at the time. In retrospect, it may have been the wrong decision. May . . . may . . . yes, *may* have made the wrong decision. But God was with me, and I knew that whatever decision I made would be the best I could do at the time, given who and where I was in my life. And he forgives me. In the stillness, I know that."

"That's another miracle of Ps 46," she continued. "The stillness inside becomes occupied by reassuring thoughts, by the love and strength of God. Fewer and fewer self-recriminations. More reassurances. There are so many who would condemn me for what I did, having an abortion; frankly, their certainty is insulting. They don't know what it is to be a young woman, alone, experiencing rape and divorce and now pregnancy."

She turned to me, her face, paled by disease, but soft in the glow of the light reflected off the ornaments. "God is with me, then and this moment. Now you know the rest of the story. And, as you might say: 'So says that great theologian, Paul Harvey.'"

"Into the maelstrom," I said quietly, quoting another great theologian, Edgar Allen Poe. All of twenty-three she had been, and 'into the maelstrom.'"

Forgiveness

"You make the best decisions you can, given who you are at the time. The Spirit walked me through the experience, so I wasn't alone. 'Be still and know that I am God!' 'The nations are in chaos, and their kingdoms crumble'—my world was in chaos, my life felt like it was crumbling in ways I had never foreseen in my young and naive years on this planet. But the good news is that God and faith and Ps 46 helps deal with the consequence of decisions, good or bad, such as the one to have an abortion, that you may well have not made in a different time and place. As I said, you do the best you can with what you've got. And always, you're forgiven; and your faith, and the discernment that comes with a personal relationship with the Spirit allows you to forgive yourself. Sin? Yes, and there are consequences. But if Jesus has forgiven me, then how can I not forgive myself? That's so important, self-forgiveness. Soon I was smiling again."

I nodded. I didn't know what to say, I hadn't heard this before. I knew only that she had been divorced. I had never asked about the details and Sharon had never offered. Her relationships before me were, in fact, comfortably vague.

Meanwhile, back at the ranch, the clock was ticking and the ALS advancing and so much still to share.

Good Boy

"I admire you," I told her many times in those final days, as I had repeatedly over three decades of marriage. "Words can't express how much I care about you, how much I love you." I thought about Ps 46 and, for me, the work of memorization and application. I had never easily memorized anything. "But I owe it to you, I think, to do this."

Deep breath, looking for that sense of calm that she always seemed to possess and was confident that I could possess with her help, the faith-guided purpose that was helping her get through the ALS.

I took a deep and calming breath. And stopped, motionless. "See, I'm getting used to it already, just like you wanted. 'Be still and know that that I am God!' And then pull from memory the passages that work for my situation."

"Good boy," she smiled, patting my arm which had been in her lap with one finger.

10

A Last Lesson

I Can't Survive ALS—But I Can

WE WERE NEARING THE end of December, and Sharon was deteriorating rapidly. I sat by her side in her room as she slept, making myself available for conversation during the short periods of consciousness that the disease allowed, weaving them around the visits of our girls. No more field trips to the Christmas tree in the living room. No more beauty of winter over the ravine. However, the small tree in her room provided a softly colored light during the night, and a symbol of the faith that mystically made ALS less frightening to her.

"It's scary, what's happening to me," she said at one point.

"Yes, it is," I agreed.

"God is with me," she rasped, the words barely audible. "I know it. His Spirit is guiding me, pushing me to focus, even now, on helping you and the girls. You now, and later, the girls through you. He helps me to stay firm in the belief that once I'm done here"—with a tremendous effort, she circled her finger—"there is so much ahead. I can't survive here with ALS, but I *will* live again. I *will* go through ALS and live again."

I nodded. "I know, sweetheart, I know."

For the most part, it was just the two of us together, our daughters occasionally from afar. I dozed in the upholstered chair next to her bed, a blanket pulled over me, waiting for her to wake. Sleep, talk, sleep, talk, sleep, talk—throughout the night, and at moments grabbed during the next day when the aides had left. Little chunks of talk, slowly and haltingly, that added up to lengthy conversations as she pushed purposefully through the ALS to fulfill her self-appointed purpose: to enable me to endure the grief of her passing and, again, find the joy that had marked our three decades together. Then, through my much changed and Spirit-driven relationships with others, especially our daughters, affect the world. Her legacy, her gift. "God is within her, she will not fall—Ps 46," I thought.

Thus was ALS conquered, through faith and purpose.

"I've gotten through today, yesterday the same way I've walked through every day of my life, through trauma and difficulties, through stupid little disagreements with you, and unforeseen crises . . ." She wiggled a finger to forestall any comment on my part, "Normal, sweetie, normal. Every relationship has stupid little arguments. Especially those couples raising kids. Everyone makes less-than-good decisions at times. But through all of the highs, the lows, the crises that were crises and the crises that turned out not to be crises, faith was part of my inner life, as was forgiveness.

"Now, faith has given me purpose: Help you to continue. Understand that the good and often great times, the crises both major and minor of everyday life, although a struggle, can be overcome by 'Be still and know . . .' Psalm 46 and its application, *Ps-46 it*, has been part of my inner life, my spiritual life since the age of seven. I had intended to discuss it with you after you retired . . ."

"When we would be lounging on a beach under an umbrella with glasses of sweet tea in our hands, watching the grandkids play," I interrupted, gently smiling. "See? I've been listening!"

"But this *stinkin' stuff* intervened," she said haltingly. "The clock is about run out."

I said nothing, just looking at her as the quiet glow of the medical devices mixed with the lights of the mini-Christmas tree in the room.

"But now . . ." her voice trailed off. "I can't survive ALS, not now. It remains a mystery disease. But I'm getting through it . . ."

"With faith and purpose," I finished. "Good stuff . . . as opposed to *stinkin' stuff.*"

She pushed on, determined to drive home her message. "Grief can destroy the years you have left," she said to me. "Grief could have destroyed me; grief over wrong decisions, grief over horrific circumstances, grief over the unfairness of life."

"And guilt, the guilt that comes with any life-threatening disease," I said, surprised by the anger behind the words. "What did I do wrong, could I have prevented this?"

"Looking back," she said, her words barely audible. "Looking for woulda-coulda. No good for you, no good for me. My illness is now. You're here now. So much of Ps 46 is in present tense for a reason: 'God *is* our refuge,' 'There *is* a river,' "God *is* within her.' Stay in the *now*. Pray in the *now*. Love me, our girls . . . *now.*"

I nodded. "I pray, but it doesn't change this: you're here, I'm here. And my prayers are fragmented, often angry, not making sense. I wish I were more eloquent, that I could put together the right combination of words to magically lift the cloud in this room, to change all this."

"He doesn't care about fancy words, about eyes open or closed. He responds to heart, prayerful heart. And your heart will know his response—whether now or ten years from now—and you will change. I know."

"How?"

"I just know. Beyond reason. It's called faith." A chuckle that ended with a gasp. "My goal right now is to help you adjust, to live with and—sounds strange—sometimes enjoy your grief, our memories. I can't survive the beast in my body, but I can survive here through you and the girls while I go on to . . . more. I'll go on to more, that's God's promise."

And she drifted off to sleep.

A LAST LESSON

So . . . So . . . So Sharon

She wanted her family to find joy. So . . . so . . . so Sharon.

No anger, no screaming, no cursing. Concentrate on others, ignore as best as possible the pain and suffering. One aide, who had cared for many terminally ill patients over the years, plunked herself down across from me in the room overlooking the ravine one evening, after getting Sharon bathed and settled for a nap. It was about two weeks before her passing. I looked up from my book. Silence.

"Everything all right in there?" I asked.

She nodded, saying nothing. I waited.

"She's so . . . sweet. Nice."

"Yes, I know,"

"In over ten years, I've never had a patient like her."

I waited, knowing where this was going. And quietly pleased, once again, that others felt the unique warmth and love of my best friend of more than three decades.

"No anger, no screaming at the unfairness of it all, no cursing. No taking her pain out on me. Most of them (hospice patients) do, you know." We sat in silence while I watched her work her way through this. As the ALS continued its course, I had scheduled healthcare workers for extra hours to assist in making Sharon as comfortable as possible. Many of them came away from her room visibly shaken, not so much by the disease, for as health workers in palliative care settings they had seen it all, but by her quiet— although weary—cheer and warmth and smiles. Despite her suffering.

She shook her head. "Sort of takes your breath away, huh?

"Yup."

Secret Sauce

Later.

"So, all of these years, all of your life, Ps 46 has been the secret sauce?" I asked.

"Yes," she said. "This approach, this *process* is, as you put it, the secret sauce," she revealed. "Guaranteed peace and discernment, a way to open your essence to the Spirit and find courage and wisdom."

"Essence?" I looked at her, a slight chuckle in my throat. "You sound like something out of the seventies. Back in the day, our day. Hippies, 'cool, man' and tie-dyed. Or New Age: aromatherapy, astrology, and healing stones. Woo woo stuff."

"Yes, essence," she said flatly, smiling and then adding, "Cool, man."

I laughed.

"The personal spiritual connection that makes you who you are. God touching you. Jesus—again, God—touching you. Your lifeforce. It doesn't matter what you call this. The Spirit will personally connect to the thoughts, the beliefs, the values, the emotions that are you. Life force, essence, Spirit—call it what you will. Close your eyes when the waters are flooding over you."

"Hey," I said, "Another Bible reference."

She brought a tremoring finger up to her lips.

"Shhhh," she said. "Don't tell anyone that I know this stuff. Saves arguments that I have never had, anyway. I have faith, regardless of what others may very loudly say about God."

I laughed and nodded. "Yes, I know you do. But the great thing about you is that it's a natural part of you, not something tacked on to impress."

Psalm 46—Oil on Troubled Waters

"I've used Psalm 46, especially the 'be still' verse, all of my life, in all situations. Stillness leads to Spirit, to Jesus as God and God as Jesus. It's worked out for me. I've had a beautiful life with you and the girls. No matter what I—we—have faced in the way of bumps, of *stinkin' stuff*, I've been blessed."

"Lot of bumps," I noted, thinking back to the hard times, the good times, the precarious times that every family faces. Unemployment, long-distance commuting, relationship issues, medical problems; you name it, we've been through it. And now, the mega-bump of all bumps, a terminal illness.

"To be expected," she replied. "Now you know about the bumps way before you came on the scene, too. And more than bumps—a whole lot of *stinkin' stuff*, just like everyone else, whether they admit it or not. But I am thankful for what I've had, what we've had together. And even now, I'm thankful for the peace that comes from the Spirit's guidance, and the knowledge that—no matter what—my life will continue, that everything will work out for me . . . and I've given you the best chance I can of creating a healthy grief, now that I've got you memorizing and using the psalm."

I turned my head slightly, looking at the lights of the mini-Christmas tree while I rested my hand on her arm. "Peace doesn't just come overnight," I observed.

"No," she said. "You have to work at it, work at the spiritual connection, and work at applying the wisdom and confidence that comes through that connection. Have faith."

Pay to Play

"One last thing," Sharon said, "and then our lessons will be over."

She turned her head partly, slowly, and painfully, fixing me with an intense gaze. "A few years before we met, I had decided that I wanted a college education. The divorce liberated me. The satisfaction I experienced by asserting myself in a bad situation—by getting out from under the thumb of a man who cared so little about my goals and was simply using me as a source of income—spilled over into the rest of my life. When I was a teenager, the teachers and counselors discouraged girls like me, with no savings and being a single mom, from going on to college. Be a hotel maid, they urged. Or work in retail. But I wanted a different life, and recognized the low bar of their expectations for what it was: the limitations of an isolated rural town, a point of view that saw women as lesser. College? Even if I weren't actively discouraged, mom and I couldn't afford it. So, I saved my money, went to a secretarial school for a couple of months, and eventually became an executive secretary in Atlanta. Hey, I made more money than I'd ever had in my life.

"But once I got a taste of that different life, my abortion and divorce behind me, I felt the urge to do even more, to find a job where I made the decisions instead of simply following in the wake of someone else. Nothing wrong with being a secretary, of course, especially since I was an executive secretary. But I wanted a college degree, a bachelor's. I planned and saved for a year, and then was accepted at a nearby state college. Between my savings, loans, and part-time fashion modeling for two large department stores, I had put together enough to become a full-time student."

"You wanted more. And were willing to work to get it."

"I borrowed as little as possible so I could pay it back, lived on a crazy strict budget. My spaghetti and butter period. I chose communication as a major, with the idea that I'd do public relations for an Atlanta hotel someday. Very specific dream."

"Good to have goals."

She nodded. "That first year was difficult. Full-time studying. Exams. Class participation. Challenging questions, discussions . . . thinking, even. Spaghetti and butter every day. Wearing oversized plaid flannel shirts and jeans. No worrying about what to wear, office etiquette. I loved it! I was a college student at last! It was fun, eye-opening, to realize that not only men made decisions; women, too. It's not how I was raised. I felt as though I had landed on another planet. I was older than the other students, in my late mid-twenties, but innocent in so many ways, in awe of the professors. They knew so much! Then, *stinkin' stuff* happened. Again."

"Always does," I noted quietly.

"I was having trouble with a required math course. The instructor had said that we could approach him at any time for help. I took him at his word, and one day waited until the classroom had emptied. I showed him the chapter of the text I was having a problem with and asked for help." She sighed. "I'll say this for him: He was direct. Sure, he said, in exchange for sex. That wasn't the word he used, actually."

My eyes narrowed. "I can imagine."

"I just looked at him. 'Pay to play,' he leered. I stood, motionless. He stepped forward, right up close to me. I could smell his breath."

"Math professor breath," I said, trying to lighten the mood in the room. "Even worse than college administrator breath, but not as bad as English professor breath."

She snickered. "He kept inching forward, invading my space. I instinctively put my hand up, pushing him back. I must have pushed too hard, because he lost his balance, falling into the lectern. Both he and the lectern fell, tangled together, and hit the floor and bounced, finally sprawling facing the floor near the front of the classroom. He turned over, looked at me, angry, started to get up."

"With or without the lectern?"

She laughed. "Without," she said. "I stepped forward. I was going to help him up—I had only wanted to push him away, and was surprised by his fall—but he thought I was going after him and quickly lay back down on the floor, one arm draped over the lectern. For what felt like forever. He was still, I was still . . . and, when he made no further attempt to stand, I turned away and walked out of the room. I thought about apologizing for his fall, but realized that he was terrified of me. So turned away, and never went back to the class. I received a failing grade, and later repeated the course at a different university. You can argue that I should have fussed, reported him to the administration. It was unfair. It was wrong. I shouldn't have to lose the credits and my tuition. But those were different times for women, and it would have been my word against his, a female student whose major accomplishment in life had been to become 'just' a secretary versus a prestigious math professor."

"It gets me angry just thinking about it," I said.

"I know. And anger mixed with despair was what I felt as I walked out of that classroom. But I went back to my apartment, closed my eyes, took a deep breath, and let the Spirit guide me. 'Be still . . .' Anger, frustration, disgust—it could have overwhelmed me but it didn't. I reached down, deep. I connected to God." Her eyes turned toward me. "Sweetie, I *felt* his Spirit. Sometimes doing nothing, just turning away from a situation, taking the consequences—unfair, yes—is the best approach. And during that time with my eyes closed, of connection, an understanding of the best path forward crept into my consciousness. Keep walking, right past this course. That's what he said. Finally, I felt that inside smile . . . and satisfaction."

She nodded at the memory. "That's what you'll need going forward. Let the grief slowly dissipate, like an early fog as the sun comes up. And then let life happen."

11

Psalm 46: Be Still, Be Loved, Be Strong

Positive and Smiling—That's Faith

FAITH MADE SHARON AN optimist. At the same time. faith gave her the strength to face the reality of her situation: ALS was slowly, steadily consuming her muscles and it was only a matter of time until she would be unable to draw a breath, despite the medical technology that surrounded her and excellent medical care at the university health center where she was a patient.

She knew that her days were numbered and, as she said with regret, "I don't like it, I hate it, but I'll enjoy my family right up until the last minute." Then came the twinkle. Always the twinkle in her eyes, sometimes shrouded by tears during that year, but a twinkle and a ghost of a smile nevertheless. "And give you advice. Good moms, wives are always ready to give advice."

She was the embodiment of the miraculous effects of faith. Faith helped her develop into a strong and independent woman over the years. Family, friends, caregivers: she inevitably responded to them with the confidence and grace that the certainty of believing in a God that inspired Ps 46, who gave her the Spirit-inspired assurance that he is "always ready to help in times of trouble."

In the death grip of ALS, faith held the bitterness and anger at bay; and as the grasp of the disease tightened, the greater the faith and the brighter her smile. Psalm 46, like a laser, focused her faith and allowed Sharon to wholeheartedly believe that "we will not fear when earthquakes come and the mountains crumble into the sea."

Positive and smiling through to the end despite "the beast in my body." This is the woman of faith whose doctors, whose caregivers considered themselves blessed to be part of her life. It's not often that a neurologist, who's seen it all in his patients, is moved to drop his world-weariness, take her shaking and increasingly lifeless hand and say, "I'm blessed to have known you." With tears in his eyes.

Blessed. Wonderful word. Around Sharon, blessings and gratitude and smiles were infectious.

A Connected Peace

Sharon had her secret sauce. Psalm 46, the way to wisdom, guidance, and strength, to putting into practice the spiritual virtues that were central to a life which, like all of our lives to some degree or another, consisted of a series of challenges, of *stinkin' stuff* to walk through. The difference, however, was that she overcame her *stinkin' stuff* without developing a chip on her shoulder, without developing an attitude that the world owes her, that she's a victim, that she's helpless. Her life had been challenging, at times horrific. Others in her shoes might have been consumed by rage; but faith and Ps 46 rescued her.

"You're hurt. You're treated unfairly. You're a victim. Okay, now, 'Be still and know' and move on," she said, remembering the past. "There will always be injustice. Get professional counseling, if that's called for. Or pray. Or talk with someone who lives right, who thinks right. Take the necessary action. But don't focus on the hurt; focus on the happiness ahead, the potential for joy. And you'll find it."

"We are 'the city of our God,' all of us and each one of us," she emphasized, plucking the words from Ps 46. "*I* am the city. And the Spirit brings me joy. So let the ALS finish its work, as it must. 'Let the oceans roar and foam,' but remember: Just as I am not alone, you are not alone."

Her joy played out in everything from her volunteer work to her regular calls and visits to her mother, in her loving notes to her friends, in her warmth and patience with her family, to her supernatural calm in the face of *stinkin' stuff*.

No big splashes, no celebrity, no framing who she was in the context of the cultural movement-of-the-moment. Her life was triumphantly simple. Steadfast love and kindness and humility. Psalm 46 and *Ps-46 it*.

She accepted that unfairness, tragedy, and suffering are part and parcel of human life. She understood that the processes and patterns for the created world had been established "beyond time and by a power beyond my understanding. But I can link to him; through his Spirit, I can get energy and love and the ability to keep on walking. God didn't give me ALS, but he has given me the perseverance to endure it . . . smiling, as best I can."

She chuckled, which came out as a hoarse whisper. "Close your eyes, begin the process, and you increase the chance of doing right. Cultivate quiet—*shalom*." She lifted her right index finger, tried to wave it, and dropped it back onto the bed, exhausted by the effort. "The power is part of us, all around us. I know we can find you peace after . . ."

". . . 'I'm gone.'" I finished her sentence. Reluctantly.

A Coffin and Hope

And so, she had—gone, from this world at least.

Later I stood, lightly touching her coffin on a windswept hillside in January at the foot of the Blue Ridge mountains. The other mourners had left.

We were alone one last time. I gently tapped the corner of her coffin, which at her insistence was a simple affair.

"I love you, sweetie."

"I know," came her voice in my head.

My imagination? Doesn't matter. Her faith, her Spirit-driven smiles and love had changed my life. *Is* changing my life. *Will* continue to change my life. Psalm 46. *Psalm-46 it.*

And when I walked slowly away from her coffin, over to the waiting car from the funeral home, it was with head up, back straight, and a ghost of a smile on my face.

Psalm 46, indeed.

"Be still and know . . ."

Epilogue

ONE OF SHARON'S LAST requests was that I deliver the eulogy at her funeral.

"You know me best, you know what I've tried to do, to say," she said.

"I don't think I can do it," I replied. "You'll have passed, and I will barely be able to tie my shoes."

"So what? Your dress shoes are loafers, no laces. Psalm 46, remember?"

Psalm-46 it to my sorrow, to our family's loss and grief . . . and I stood—in my loafers—to deliver her eulogy in the chapel:

> For the next few, very few minutes I'm going to talk to you about Sharon—wife, mother, daughter, friend. Or, I should say, awesome mother, patient wife, caring daughter, nutty about abandoned kitties and God . . . not necessarily in that order.
>
> When you talk about Sharon you talk kindness and faith and love. When I sat down last night to talk with my daughters about this eulogy, they said, "Dad, I don't know how you'll do it—when you think about it, she was so unreal." Unreal, yes. She always found a way to smile. And love. Quite unreal in the face of the cynicism of our world.
>
> And so, I did what Sharon would do. I had spent almost thirty-three years with Sharon, and those years shaped this eulogy and my faith. "Set the stage," she painfully, agonizingly tapped out on her iPad. One finger worked. Barely. "Help the girls get beyond the grief by

setting the stage for the next part of their lives." And so, I reached down deep, found a smile, and wrote this.

I can certainly tell you some anecdotes, funny things that have happened, especially when you're raising two girls. But as I think about this or that incident, about all the turns and twists over the years . . . well, all I can do is shake my head in wonder at her patience. And love.

But I shouldn't be surprised. This is the woman whose doctor left me a voicemail the day she passed that said, "I'm blessed to have been able to take care of your wife and we'll miss her." Whose respiratory equipment representative emailed that "she was one of the most beautiful women I have ever met." And whose neurologist took her shaking hand and, tears in his eyes, said, "I'm blessed to have known you."

She had that effect on people. Sharon smiled; even terminally ill, she smiled. Often with joy, lately tinged with sadness, but Sharon smiled because, bottom line, she was quite content to be rooted in God, with simply being nice and thereby reaping the spiritual rewards of loving relationships with family and friends. As she said, "You know, Bible stuff."

Perhaps the girls are thinking: Awwwww, dad— so not cool. Well, certainly not where I was born and worked, New York City. But this eulogy, Sharon's story, is God's story. It's the story he writes in each of us, there for the digging.

Sharon walked with Christ. She lived Christ in her love, her relationships. Her devotion to her children. To her husband. To her mom. We were, unapologetically, her life's work, all with the Spirit as her guide.

"I'm not afraid," she told me as her time here was drawing to a close, "Just sad that I can't be there to take care of all of you. Jesus suffered—and look what he did? 'Be still and know God.' Listen to the silence, and faith will make a difference in your lives and of those around you, even after I'm gone."

We can rejoice because there was so much love in our home, led by a woman who found a way to smile, at least a part of every day. She lived love. In the Halloween costumes she made for our girls, in the homework she helped them with, in the endless trips over the mountain to sit with her mom, in good works, and in her patience with me. Especially her patience with me.

I could go on and on—but what I would be describing are the biblical virtues, the spiritual forces that were personal and central to her life. No big splashes, no celebrity. Her life was triumphantly simple: just steadfast love and kindness and humility. All flowing from God's Spirit.

Sharon gave to others as a matter of course. Her heart, her soul played out in everything from her volunteer work to her regular calls to her mom (honor your father and mother, right? "Bible stuff," as she would say, from Exodus), to her loving notes to her friends, to her warmth and patience with her family.

And even in this, in the midst of a brutal and cruel disease she kept "Christ in my heart" was how she put it. "Be still and know . . ." That, in turn, allowed her a fulfilling peace, not something you usually associate with ALS. It is a disease of horror and for most ALS sufferers, despair quickly sets in.

But with Sharon there was quiet sadness—no despair. Faith kept despair at bay. As she wrote in her journal, "There is a time in your life when you have to learn to let go, of the ones I love, of possessions, of control. I'm learning—I'm sad, but I'm happy—because they'll do just fine and I'll see them again."

This is the woman who, little more than twelve months ago, got the news that two years of strange things going on with her body was, in fact, a terminal illness, a hellish disease that no one in the medical community knows how you get—but everyone knows how it ends.

And what did she do after hearing the diagnosis? She wrapped her arms around me and sobbed, "I don't want to leave you alone. I don't want to leave you alone." She would die—but I'm the one she worried about.

And then she proceeded toward the end of her life with a single purpose: Make sure her husband, her daughters would continue on . . . and put grief behind them. A woman with a purpose.

Doing God was as natural as breathing to Sharon. And more so toward the end, when her breathing faltered but her connection to the Spirit kept going. Even in her suffering she continued to love, to smile, encouraging her girls, loving her cats and her husband (in that order).

"God is good," she said, and I know for many that seems improbable. Are you kidding? Did you see what happened to her? Yup—in fact, I had a front row seat. I saw suffering, but I also saw joy and faith and a thousand and one kindnesses in that last year. And I saw her never waver in her belief in a happy ending, the ending we are all promised in our walk with God, with Jesus, with the beyond-natural spiritual forces that Sharon connected to.

This evil robbed her of everything; everything that all of us in here take for granted (breathing, walking, speaking, hugging, swallowing . . . everything). Yet, Sharon was firm in the belief that God didn't bring this evil upon her. He didn't plan for this to happen to her. Life in a world in which evil and disease and corruption are woven throughout resulted in this.

How that works, why—that's a discussion for another day. As she said so many times, don't ask *why* life often hurts, as Job did in her beloved Bible. Count your blessings, she said, and then enjoy the source of those blessings. God. Another lesson of Job, the overriding one. It's sufficient to say, as she did, that in this world *stuff happens,* "*stinkin' stuff,*" as our young daughters described it. But amidst sorrow and suffering, Sharon was determined to have conversations; to pray in the stillness of her room and her personal relationship with God's Spirit; and to use the evil of her illness as an opportunity to bring the glorious power of faith to bear in the lives of her family.

So many times, by her bed I'd say, "You're my forever love." And in the end, in the small hours of Tuesday morning, when I gently placed her back in bed after attending to her needs, her smile still worked.

"I love you," she rasped.

"You're my forever love," I whispered.

"Remember," she gasped. "Be still."

And she smiled. Again, always. That smile remained when, three hours later, she had gone on to explore the other side of that spiritual connection that comes through the stillness. To her, life was a series of miracles.

That she could still smile at the end: I'll take that miracle any day.

As time has passed, I have changed. For the better. The grief is there, but overshadowed by joyful memories, and a positive way of living. Life experienced in newly fulfilling ways.

Love does that, you know . . . which was her point exactly.

The power of the word of God does that, you know . . . again, her point exactly.

More God stuff, as Sharon put it.

Great stuff. It works.

"Be still and know . . ."

As promised.

Sharon

www.ingramcontent.com/pod-product-compliance
Lightning Source LLC
Chambersburg PA
CBHW060311100426
42812CB00003B/744